The Romance of Balboa Park

To him who, in the love of Nature,
Holds Communion with her visible forms,
She speaks a various language.
For his gayer hours, she has a voice of
    gladness
And a smile, and eloquence of beauty
And she glides into his darker musings
With a mild and tender sympathy
That steals away their sadness, ere he is
    aware.

William Cullen Bryant

The Romance of Balboa Park

FOURTH EDITION, REVISED

by
FLORENCE CHRISTMAN

*"The first glimpses one catches of its
architectural aggregate, and particularly of the
tower, are like a vision of romance."*

EUGEN NEUHAUS, from
The San Diego Garden Fair

San Diego Historical Society
P.O. Box 81825
San Diego, California 92138
©1985 by Florence Christman

Designed by Thomas L. Scharf

Published in 1985 by the
San Diego Historical Society

Second Printing, 1988

Library of Congress Cataloging in Publication Data
Christman, Florence.
  The Romance of Balboa Park
  Bibliography: p.
  Includes index.
  1. Balboa Park (San Diego, Calif)—History.
2. San Diego (Calif.)—Parks—History. I. Title
F869.S22C48 1985   979.4'98   85-2368
ISBN 0-918740-03-7

Printed in the United States of America
by Crest Offset Printing Company
National City, California

Unless otherwise noted all photographs
used throughout are from the San Diego
Historical Society's Title Insurance and Trust Collection

Cover photo courtesy of the City of San Diego, Phil Binks

Table Of Contents

Preface

The story of Balboa Park is a story of men and women, of their concern for the beauty and improvement of San Diego and especially of how their leadership, and, on many occasions, their large monetary gifts, have served to develop one of the great parks in the entire nation.

From 1850 early San Diegans experienced some misgivings over land for schools, parks and other public use. Their concern was justified. There was a reckless disposal of public lands. By 1867 the most desirable lands were in private hands. Pueblo lots of 160 acres would be dealt out with a "prodigal generosity." A report of the sale of lands of June 1867 told of two lots of 160 acres which had sold for $11.00 each, less than 7ᶜ an acre.

At the urging of those early citizens on February 15, 1868 Ephraim W. Morse presented a modest resolution to set aside two 160 acre parcels of pueblo lands for a park. Joshua Sloane was secretary of the board of trustees: the result of the vote was not recorded.

But on May 26th E.W. Morse and Alonzo Horton brought in the recommendation that 1400 acres be set aside, "to be for a park." That action was voted affirmatively.

For the next few years little mention of this park reservation is found in the press. However, on March 29, 1882 the *San Diego Union* states:

San Diego has wisely set aside a public park of 1400 acres occupying the high mesa overlooking the town and bay; this ground apparently unfit for any private uses may yet constitute the glory of a flourishing seaport city, at present occupied only by a pest house and the skeleton of a commodious school house, it may yet add to its magnificent views.

No mention is made of improvement of the park. But two years later on December 23, 1884:

The present is an excellent season to take steps toward improving and beautifying San Diego and vicinity: it is time that improvements be made on the grounds which have been laid out for a park; at present there is no attraction for visitors except the mild and healing climate; and the suggestions which have been made by several of late, that a commencement be made with a view of permanently improving the park is one that should meet with the unqualified approval and the hearty support of all.

And on the following day:

Money judiciously expended in making public improvements, such as the improvement of the grounds selected as a city park, and in other ways making San Diego more attractive will bring a reward a hundredfold in time to come.

On Christmas Day 1884:

Every resident and every property holder who desires the welfare of San Diego will be pleased when the work of improving the park is actually begun.

And one final example three days later:

Editor Union: This year being so favorable for planting trees, I would suggest that something be done right off to develop a part of the plot of land reserved for a city park. When a stranger approaches our city from the bay, he admires the scenery of the hills and mountains spread out before his eye; but at the same time there is something which does not please, it is the want of vegetation which makes the country appear desert like: I would propose to commence this season with a few hundred trees—say eucalyptus—in the neighborhood of the new school building.

From 1900 on, items about the city park increased, and beginning about 1900 until today seldom a day's paper misses some if not several references to the park.

G. Aubrey Davidson in 1909 suggested an exposition for the benefit of the city and the park to celebrate the great achievement of the Panama Canal; the idea was adopted and the fair incorporated; all this before the park had a name. But in 1910, a contest for a name was won by Harriet Phillips; the name Balboa—the Spanish explorer first to glimpse the Pacific Ocean. George Marston's name is resplendent throughout the early development of the park. Julius Wangenheim, spurred to action, made the initial move to officially start park improvement. Kate Sessions was there with her splendid persuasion in planting and landscape. She is purported to have said, ''I would rather be remembered for one beautiful tree than for all the marble in the world.'' She is well remembered by a grateful city.

Many noted architects walked through the history of Balboa Park. Samuel Parsons left his mark on the park because San Diego leaders would have the best. Later an architect dreamed beautiful buildings of Spanish Colonial design and twenty years later another one favored a different era of historical architecture. Eminent local architects were W. Templeton Johnson who brought two beautiful buildings, the San Diego Museum of Art and the Natural History Museum; and San Diego's Sam Hamill whose renovation of the House of Hospitality delights all who visit there.

An inspired leader, Bea Evenson died October 31, 1981. But, restoration of Balboa Park buildings will continue assured by the devoted performance of the Committee of 100 of which she was founding president.

In recent years other architects have touched Balboa Park: Mosher and Drew conceived the west wing of the San Diego Museum of Art; George W. Devine created the Timken Art Gallery; Louis Bodmer and George C. Hatch prepared plans for the Reuben H. Fleet Space Theater and Science Center; the Ninteman Company carefully removed art forms from the Food and Beverage Building (now Casa del Prado) and the Electric Building (now Casa de Balboa), thus making possible restoration as they first appeared in 1915. A large gift from Helen Edison assured the replacement of the Old Globe Theatre—destroyed by arson.

Civic organizations such as the Sierra Club and the Citizens Coordinate for Century 3 stress preserving land use. Courageous leader of the latter group, Dr. Clare Crane, made a valiant effort to return land dedicated to the park by locating the new Naval Hospital elsewhere, but an official in Washington D.C. decreed otherwise.

How well Lew Scarr defined the essence of the park in the *San Diego Union,* January 1, 1969:

A park is unlike any other asset in the city. It is not a building, nor a production line, nor a warm breeze. A park is a living, growing thing that will die if the will of the people dies, or it will flourish as much as they want it to.

Florence Christman
January, 1985

*Florida Street canyon,
c. 1900*

*City Park at Sixth and
Date streets, c. 1903*

A PARK IS CREATED AND EVOLVES

The story of Balboa Park began in Spain in 1789 when King Carlos III signed a guide or plan by which land surveys were made to establish towns, or pueblos, as they were called in Spanish California. Such surveys divided "Real Property" into three categories. One of these was designated "Commercial land held for the people, in common, for pasturage or for recreational purposes." The site of what is now Balboa Park was selected from land in this class, and because of this derivation the park may very well be one of the oldest tracts of land in the United States designated for recreational usage.

The title to this area was transferred from Spain to Mexico in 1822. Under the Mexican government the Presidio of San Diego organized the first municipal government, and this took over many of the duties formerly performed by the military organization.

The first primary election was held December 18, 1834. Thirteen electors were chosen. Three days later these men met and cast thirteen votes for Juan María Osuna for alcalde. This was called San Diego's first "landslide" election. José M. Marron and Juan B. Alvarado were elected counsellors and Henry D. Fitch, legal advisor. On January 1, 1835 the new officials took office and San Diego—population 432—became a pueblo.

As one of the first official acts, the new authorities applied to the Mexican government for a grant of land from the public domain, to which under the colonial laws of Spain and Mexico, San Diego, now a pueblo, was legally entitled for use and benefits of the citizens. Mexico responded that same year with a grant of 47,000 acres. No survey or boundaries were given for the next ten years. In 1845 Mexico, through the Department of California, gave Henry D. Fitch orders to survey and make a map of the pueblo grant. Three years later, under the treaty ending the Mexican War, the area became a part of the United States, and in 1850, of the state of California.

In 1851 when San Diego was incorporated under the first state legislature, it was the Fitch map and survey which established the boundaries of San Diego. This "pueblo" grant had a secondary survey and map made by John C. Hayes in 1858. The results agreed in practically all points with the Fitch map.

In 1868 San Diego was a town of 2,301 citizens and 915 houses. Real estate showed a value of $2,828,000. Citizens of San Diego asked the Board of Trustees to have pueblo lands set aside for a park. On February 15, 1868, Ephraim Morse presented a resolution to the trustees requesting that they reserve two, one hundred and sixty acre tracts of city lands for the purpose of securing a suitable park for the inhabitants of San Diego.

The resolution was adopted by trustees J.S. Mannasse, president, Thomas B. Bush and Ephraim W. Morse. President Mannasse named Morse and Bush to choose the most suitable location, and to plot this on an official map. Later, probably in April, a new Board of Trustees was elected. José Guadalupe Estudillo was President, with Marcus Schiller and Joshua Sloane serving with him. Apparently Thomas Bush supported the park movement, but he took no part in the selection of a site. Ephraim Morse took a man destined to become San Diego's premiere city founder, Alonzo Horton, with him to look for a park locale.

Pueblo lands had been selling for as little as seven cents per acre, partly because the trustees were eager to place more land on private tax lists. When Morse and Horton went over the possible locations, they considered how worthless the land was, and that the original request for 320 acres would be inadequate for a park. Therefore, they set about choosing a much larger space. The area they finally chose was all but square in shape, but for a forty-acre plot at the extreme southwest corner of the land they wanted. On February 13, 1868, this plot had been sold to Isabella Carruthers for $175.

In a letter written by Ephraim Morse to Alonzo Horton on August 27, 1904, he stated that he

Thomas Bush, c. 1870

Alonzo Horton, c. 1867

and Horton really located the park; that Horton stood by him until the park was "clinched"; that no one did as much as Horton to save it. Morse made the decision to increase the area from 320 to 1,400 acres of pueblo lands and could well spare that number for a park."

On May 26, 1868, it was moved and seconded that Lots 1131, 1130, 1129, 1135, 1136, 1137, and the vacant part of Lots 1144, 1143, 1142, "be for a park." Trustee Schiller made the motion; it was seconded by Estudillo and Sloane. At the time the estimated value of the tract was $6,000. Today the remaining 1,074 acres of Balboa Park are estimated to have a value of more than a billion dollars.

The real leader of the park movement was Ephraim Morse, but he had the full support of Alonzo Horton, Joseph S. Mannasse and Thomas Bush. The park was thus established just one year after Alonzo Horton had founded San Diego's "New Town" (the site of the city's present downtown).

This dedication of a park by San Diego precedes, by two years, a similar action by San Francisco in providing for Golden Gate Park, and is second in the nation in the establishment of a large park. New York City is considered to be first in dedicating Central Park in 1858.

Early Leaders In Park History

Ephraim Morse had been a farmer and teacher in Amesbury, Massachusetts. He came to San Francisco during the Gold Rush, and to San Diego in 1850. He was a versatile man of many interests. He was at various times a merchant, a deputy sheriff and City Treasurer from 1858-59 and 1861-63. He was a town trustee, and in that capacity had been instrumental in the sale of land to Alonzo Horton. Later he helped Horton plan and build New Town. He was associated with the Bank of San Diego, first in the city; this bank later merged with the Consolidated National Bank. He was also affiliated with the San Diego Savings Bank. He and James M. Pierce built the Pierce-Morse building at Sixth and F streets, and with Thomas Whaley and R.H. Dalton built the Morse, Whaley, Dalton Block on Fifth Street between D and F streets.

In 1871 Morse represented San Diego in Washington concerning pueblo lands. He was instrumental in bringing the Santa Fe Railroad to San Diego and served as a director of the San Diego and Gila Railroad. Of all of his public offices, his interest in the park was perhaps his greatest service. He stood at all times for its preservation and improvement. He was a member of the school board when the first public school was opened in 1865. A widower, Morse defended San Diego's first teacher, Mary Chase Walker, in a famous incident that is one of the tales of the history of Old Town. He later married Miss Walker.

Some historians feel that Ephraim Morse should be recognized as the founder of Balboa Park because he inaugurated the movement for the park reservation.

Thomas Bush had been trained as a bookbinder in Philadelphia. He had prospected for gold in Lower California and in 1869 had a store in Old Town. Of Irish ancestry, he was a school trustee, a town trustee, sold lands for Alonzo Horton, and "he served as secretary of the newly formed Pioneer Society." He was in real estate for himself, and became postmaster in 1868. At the time of moving the seat of government from Old Town to New San Diego, he favored Old Town, and this was never forgotten. Nevertheless he bought ten acres of land between First and A streets and Sixth and A, and his home was at the latter location. Although he was not an attorney, he was appointed to fill the unexpired term of Julio Osuna as Judge, and served in this capacity for eight years. A friend, meeting him on the street one day said, "Judge, your hat and coat are mighty dusty," to which Bush responded. "So they are, but not near as dry as my throat."

Joseph P. Mannasse was born in Prussia and came to San Diego in 1853 where he operated a store. Beginning modestly, he prospered and became a large dealer. In 1856 he entered into partnership with Marcus S. Schiller and established a lumber yard at Atlantic and E streets. Together they bought and stocked the Encinitas Rancho.

They suffered extensive reverses during the great drought of 1870, and in the Old Town Fire of 1872. They laid out and sold the Manasse-Schiller addition. Later Mannasse became a collector and broker. His interest in public affairs was a dominant trait. He served several terms as trustee, and was president when Horton made his purchase of city land. He married Hannah Schiller, sister of his partner. Small in stature, he was affectionately called "Mannasse Chico" or "Mannasita."

José Estudillo was one of the most prominent citizens of San Diego's early days. He served as County Treasurer from 1864-1875, as a City Trustee, and as a California State Treasurer for one term. For a time he was cashier in the Consolidated National Bank. A story is told that a real estate agent was adamant in his insistence to procure a choice view location (now Marston Point) in the park. When Estudillo insisted that

the land was set aside for a park and was not for sale the man gave up and in disgust called Estudillo a "subborn old barnacle." Now, Estudillo's knowledge of English was far from perfect — he was of proud Spanish heritage and was not accustomed to name calling. He promptly challenged his caller to a duel. As the time grew near Estudillo thought he should find out the meaning of "barnacle." Upon learning that he was compared to a tenacious little sea animal which could scarcely be moved from its position he felt the term rather appropriate and the duel was cancelled.

Marcus Schiller was born in Prussia on October 2, 1819. At age seventeen he came to America — to San Francisco in 1853. Three years later, broken in health and discouraged, he came to San Diego. Here he quickly regained his health and his outlook. He was a town trustee from 1860-61 and again in 1868. He aided in the establishment of the park; was superintendent of schools from 1868 to 69; was a stockholder and director of the San Diego and Gila Railroad. His business interests with Joseph P. Mannasse have been described.

Joshua Sloane was perhaps the most colorful character of the early park leaders. Many stories are written about him. He was a native of Ireland and came from a good family. He moved to San Diego in the early 1850s, and clerked in the store owned by Ephraim Morse. In 1858 he was appointed deputy postmaster; the next year he became a postmaster. He was at political variance with the majority of the people of San Diego when his term as postmaster was about to expire, and a petition was circulated protesting his reappointment in an effort to win this political favor for one of the predominant party.

When the letter containing the petition was deposited in the post office, Sloane's curiosity was aroused by its appearance and address. He opened the letter and read the enclosure. Then with all coolness, he cut off the remonstrance, wrote on a similar piece of paper an endorsement of his work and petition for his reappointment, pasted the signatures below this and forwarded the altered enclosure in a new envelope. The people of San Diego were sorely puzzled that their almost unanimous petition passed unheeded. This remained a mystery until Sloane himself told the story years later.

In politics, he became known for his activity for the Republican party and for this service he was made Collector of the Port in 1861. He served only one term. A famous story of those days was to the effect that he appointed his dog, Patrick, Deputy Collector and carried him on the payroll.

His greatest service to San Diego was undoubtedly his work for the park. He was secretary to the Board of Trustees at the time the question of setting aside the park came up. He was one of the earliest, most tireless and most earnest advocates of a large park. One of his friends said, "He was the man who first proposed a big park here and he urged it on the trustees till they let him have his way. There were people here who wanted to cut it down in size, but due to Sloane's efforts, this was not done. He stood like a bull dog over that park, and some day people will be grateful to him for doing so. His mission here seemed to be, 'SAVE THAT PARK,' and he did it."

Alonzo Horton was born at Union, Connecticut on October 24, 1813, of Puritan stock. He was a descendant of Barnabas Horton, who came with the Pilgrims in 1635. In 1851 he located in California, seeking a climate to benefit his health. For a time he worked in the mines in the northern part of the state, but he made a fortune by cutting ice in the mountain regions and shipping this to the coastal areas. On April 15, 1867, Horton landed at the wharf near the foot of H Street, (now Market) in San Diego. He had heard of San Diego through a parlor lecture in San Francisco. He bought much of what is now downtown San Diego for twenty-seven and a half cents an acre.

Returning to San Francisco he told his wife he was going to sell his furniture store stock, which he owned there, and in three days go to San Diego to build a city. She told him he was crazy. Everyone else thought so too, but he laid out New Town, subdivided commercial and residential properties, and built homes. He made as much as $20,000 a day from the sale of the land. Yet he was generous with his land. He gave lots to groups for churches, and offered a prize to the church first completed. The prize was won by the First Baptist Church at Tenth and E streets in the fall of 1868. The church still has the bell which Horton presented to it.

In 1869 Horton said to his friend Felsenheld, who was city-bred and experienced in business affairs, "Dave, what we have to have is a Chamber of Commerce." "What," said Fels, "A Chamber of Commerce in this miserable little village that hasn't a sign of any commerce? It's absurd." "That's just it," said Horton. "We need a Chamber of Commerce to get the commerce." One was organized, and Alonzo Horton was the first treasurer.

At an early age Horton said, "My principle is to be as happy as I can every day; to try to make everyone else as happy as I can and to try to make no one unhappy."

Horton was the first citizen to ask the Board of Trustees to establish a city park in 1867, he helped select the park's site and determine its size, and he went to Sacramento in 1871 to defend the park at a time when local land-grabbers were trying to reduce its size.

At the west gate to Balboa Park is a plaque placed there in 1928 when George Marston was Park Commissioner. It reads: "Balboa Park, To commemorate the foresight and civic wisdom of the founders of Balboa Park, this tablet is erected by the people of San Diego. On May 26, 1868, on the petition of Alonzo F. Horton and Ephraim W. Morse these pueblo lands were dedicated by the trustees of the city, José Estudillo, Joshua Sloane, Marcus Schiller, to be forever a public park. In the year 1928 they gratefully honor the memory of these citizen officials."

Sixty-three years later, E.L. Hardy, President of San Diego State College, speaking in the House of Hospitality, said of these early park leaders: "One, Estudillo, a son of New Spain of the sierras, the mesas, the vales, the second, Schiller, a son of the plains of Russia with his ancestral and racial memories; the third, Sloane, son of Ireland, lured by the westward bearing trail to the Pacific, were responding to the urge of a deep human instinct, the instinct for room, for space, for green expanse and shadowy vistas. And so they set aside in San Diego a tract and noble estate — to be for a park. "Dr. Hardy spoke on behalf of the charter of 1931 which provided mandates for maintenance of the park and by which he said, "The petition of Father Horton and the action of trustees Estudillo, Schiller and Sloane were confirmed."

Park Confirmed — City Gives Away Acres!

As the law was in 1868, the trustees of San Diego were responsible to the state legislature, hence the act of May 1868 must be confirmed by the state government. This was done on February 4, 1870, with an Act to Insure the Permanency of the Park Reservation. The bill said in part: "These lands (lots by number) are to be held in trust forever by the municipal authorities of said city for the purpose of a park."

In 1903, Mary B. Coulston wrote, "In recent years a growing realization of the unusual beauty of site, space and unique features for a great park . . . together with the conclusive action of the legislature have all operated to preserve the park from attachment and division." However, in 1871 there had been a conspiracy to repeal the legislation which upheld the park dedication of May 26, 1868. Some city officials and others were involved. They proposed to rush through the legislature a bill to rescind the Act of February

1870 in order to "grab" this valuable land. But it happened that a San Diego resident, in Sacramento at the time, learned what was afoot. This information and threat were rushed to San Diego. Intense publicity and indignation followed. George Marston, Thomas Nesmith, Dan Cleveland, Mat Sherman and others organized and secured 366 signatures on a plea to keep the park intact. Sent to Sacramento, these served to kill the bill. The original of this petition and the list of names are among the historic papers at the San Diego Historical Society's Research Archives.

On December 2, 1887, the San Diego Board of Trustees granted Bryant Howard, Ephraim W. Morse, Charles Hamilton and Moses A. Luce — who were associated with the Consolidated National Bank — one hundred acres of City Park between Pound and Powder House Canyons for a charitable institution. These men built a Children's Home and set out trees on the grounds. The failure of the Consolidated National Bank in 1893 prevented them from furthering their plans.

Also in 1887, the town trustees gave the Women's Home Association five acres in the park at 1365 Sixteenth Street where the group built a home for indigent women. When the home burned this was converted to a Children's Home and so it functioned until the route chosen for a crosstown freeway forced its removal.

San Diego Government

How the town was governed in early days is well explained in Smythe's *History of San Diego:* "After the abolition of the city charter in 1852, San Diego was administered by three trustees. The boundaries of the city were defined between 1868 and 1870. In 1868 a new charter was adopted, and in 1872 the trustees were increased from three to five. The city was now 6th class. In 1887 it became 4th class. In December of 1888 there was an election of freeholders to form a new charter. On the following March 3rd, the new charter was adopted by the city and it was ratified by the legislature on March 16, 1889. The new charter became effective the following 6th of May.''

This charter provided for a mayor, the first time since 1852. (The president of the board of trustees had been called the mayor by courtesy.) Provision was made for a city attorney, a treasurer and a tax collector. The legislative branch was a Board of Delegates, two for each ward, and eighteen members in all. Also, a Board of Aldermen was elected at large. On March 1, 1906, the legislative body of aldermen and delegates was abolished; a change brought about by another change of charter in late 1905. The City Council was reduced to nine members.

The Development Of A Great Park

From 1868 to 1889 the park remained in its native state. The area was covered with cactus and chaparral. There were no trees, Coyotes, rabbits, bobcats and squirrels lived there. Rattlesnakes were everywhere. Many wild flowers were native to the park. Some of these were pansies, violets, monkey flower or mimulus, mallows, penstamens, hyacinths and white popcorn.

In 1873 a water company was organized and drilled a well at Palm Canyon. Here a subterranien stream was tapped at 300 feet. This produced 54,000 gallons of water per hour. Two concrete reservoirs were constructed on opposite mesas above the canyon. A pound was located in Palm Canyon in the southwest corner of the park now covered by the Cabrillo Freeway. To enforce a fence law, stray horses and cattle were rounded up and kept, at the owner's expense, when they were caught wandering about the city streets.

In 1882 a pest house occupied a spot near Sixth and Upas streets. A Mr. Hogue was in charge—"he was nurse, cook, and bottle washer." When no one was a patient in the pest house, he dispensed liquor downtown or at his half-way house east of town. When San Diego established the "Poor Farm," the pest house was moved there as an isolation ward.

In 1889 Dr. J.P. La Fevre, a practicing physician, organized a tree-planting club of about thirty members. Each one donated one dollar per month for the planting of eucalyptus trees on the west side of the park. Later many of these trees were victims of a severe drought, but some lived through this dry period. Also, in 1889, town people began to take an interest in the park. The Ladies Annex, an Auxiliary of the Chamber of Commerce, under the leadership of Mrs. Ben Lake, raised $500. With this money they planted a narrow strip on the west side from Juniper to Palm Street. Kate Sessions, San Diego's famous horticulturist, supervised this planting. At this time the 1,400 acres, barren, refuse-ridden except for these isolated efforts, had not even been named. But 1889 marks the beginning of the planting and the transformation into the park as we see it today.

The Impact Of Kate Sessions

Kate O. Sessions, who lived her eighty-three years unmarried, has nevertheless been called in all fondness, the "Mother of Balboa Park." The name was given to her during the 1935 Exposition in San Diego, when a day was set aside on January 31 to honor her.

She was born on Nob Hill in San Francisco on November 8, 1857. When she was six years of age her parents moved to a farm near Lake Merritt. She completed high school in Oakland and for a graduation gift, was given a trip to Hawaii. There she saw in profusion the red flowers which as a child she had copied in drawings without knowing that they were Poinsettias. In 1881 she graduated from the University of California at Berkeley where her major area of interest was Natural Science. Her essay for graduation was entitled, "The Natural Sciences as a Field for Women's Labor."

Asked once how she began her life-long interest in plants, she said, "I was always started: I grew up in a garden." When she was two years old her obsession was to pick flowers. At six years, she was using the hoe, and her father's cabbages were her first victims.

How San Diego came to have this remarkable woman, at a time when her influence was especially useful, is an interesting story.

Kate enrolled in a business college in San Francisco where she met and became a warm friend of Rosa Smith (later Mrs. Carl Eigenmann of San Diego). Rosa's father was a member of the San Diego School Board. He had written his daughter asking her to find a teacher for the high school. Rosa at once begged Kate to take this position. Miss Sessions said she knew little about teaching, but she would give it a try. She came to San Diego in 1883 as Vice-Principal and Eighth grade teacher at the Old Russ School. The Russ Lumber Company had put up a single building to house all high school classes, in place of a little building on B Street. Kate proved to be a wonderful teacher, but after a year and a half she found that her health would not allow her to continue in the teaching field.

Coronado was beginning to develop at this

Kate Sessions' City Park nursery

Kate Sessions, c. 1900

18

time and in 1885 Miss Sessions started a nursery there, growing plants and cut flowers which she sold through her sales yard and at her floral shop located at Fifth and C Streets in San Diego. In 1892 when the Coronado property had become too valuable for a nursery, Miss Sessions asked the City Council for a lease on thirty acres of the City Park in the area of Sixth and Upas. In lieu of rent she agreed to plant 100 trees each year in the park, and would also give the city 300 trees to use in other areas. The city entered into the plan and for years she planted trees in the park.

In Balboa Park today, the finest old trees stand in vigorous health and beauty because of Kate Sessions. These were started largely from seed imported from Australia, Asia, South America, Spain, Lower California and New England. Notable among these are the Monterey cypress, Torrey pines, cork oaks, pepper trees and eucalyptus. The beautiful jacaranda tree is one of her importations. From the time of Miss Sessions' arrival in San Diego, she created an interest in a general program of planting and beautifying the city. She had an enlivening personality; she drew people to her and made them captive to her love and interest toward plants.

In 1900 Miss Sessions accompanied botanist T.S. Brandegee and a party who went on mules all the way down to Baja California in search of a new type of palm tree. There they found a fan palm which was named Erythea Brandegeei, in honor of the botanist. She brought back three small plants and many seeds, and in a short time 250 of these trees were planted in the park.

In 1904 the work of developing the park progressed to the point of needing the area in which Kate had her nursery. Some years later she remarked to a friend, with her wry smile, that she paid her rent to the city by planting trees, and ironically, the park gained such impetus that the City Council invited her to take her commercial nursery out of the park without even waiting for her lease to expire.

She bought and leased property in Mission Hills between Stephens, Lewis and Lark streets and the Canyon leading into Mission Valley. Here she stayed for twenty-four years.

John D. Spreckels had started his electric car line in San Diego and Miss Sessions asked him to bring the line to her nursery. Spreckels agreed to do this providing she would get Lewis and Washington Streets widened. Alice Rainford described how she and Kate drove by horse and buggy from house to house to get petitions signed for the street work. In many instances it meant owners giving the city a few feet of their lots. Finally the two had the last signature needed; the streets were widened and the car line was extended to Stephens Street. Kate was the first customer. Spreckels soon gave her a pass since she

had the one commercial investment in the area.

In 1910 when the downtown plaza was developed, it was Kate Sessions who furnished and supervised the planting of the palm trees.

The Mission Hills area thrived in plantings. Many beautiful palm trees in that area came from her nursery, and she tells of planting with her own hands two rows of palms on Randolph Street. She was generous to her neighbors in other ways; she was known to pay street assessments for some who otherwise might have lost their property.

Through an arrangement by some of her friends, she was able to make a seven months' visit to Europe in 1925. *California Garden,* San Diego's horticulture magazine, in which her writings appeared regularly, kept a running account of her journey. In February there was an account of her departure; March and April numbers gave a lively account of her trip across the United States. In May she reached Italy; in June it was "K.O.S. in Gay Paree," and the July magazine recounted her stay in England.

From this trip she introduced new plants. Among these were the mesembryanthemums and heathers from the Lao Martola Botanical Gardens in northern Italy. She was taken seriously ill some time later, due to over-working in an important flower show in Encinitas. When she recovered, her friends proposed a dinner in her honor. Publicity was given through *California Garden.* When Kate heard of this, she sent word to the editor to come and see her; she made it clear to him that if she were to be pleased, it would be with no banquet, but rather by creating an agave and aloes garden. C.I. Jerabek designed and landscaped the garden. Labor was furnished by the W.P.A. The garden was dedicated March 23, 1935. Mary Greer, representing the San Diego Floral Association, presented the garden to the city. George Marston, in accepting for the city, said, "Botanically speaking, I would call Miss Sessions a perennial, evergreen and everblooming." In 1928 she established a nursery in Pacific Beach. After her death in 1940 and during World War II the area of her nursery became war housing. Near the road, stood a beautiful tipu or tipuana tree, native of South America and planted by Kate Sessions. Widening of that road — Balboa Avenue — was being planned when an alert Pacific Beach Woman's Club discovered that the Kate Sessions tree was to be sacrificed. At once they aroused the community to action. A petition to the state was initiated to make the corner about the tree a state landmark to honor the famous resident of that area. The women won. The engineers changed the course of Balboa Avenue, the tree was saved and on July 7th, 1961 State Historical Landmark No. 764 was dedicated. The *San Diego Union* of September 22, 1962 said: "Whenever a body of bright earnest

Cabrillo Canyon, c. 1908

Cabrillo Canyon "freeway," c. 1903

women, representative of the intelligence and culture of a community, undertakes to promote a great public improvement, the task is likely to be performed speedily and well.''

In 1939 Miss Sessions taught a class called Practical Gardening and Landscape Design for the Extension Division, University of California. Students of her class have said that she considered plants as possessing almost human feelings and instincts. She would say: "Now you take a vine. It will keep on growing until it finds something to climb. You must approach your planting from the plant's point of view. Does it like a south exposure? Or does it yearn for a northern one? Does it prefer sun or shade?''

Perhaps her greatest thrill was recognition which came to her in 1939. The American Genetic Association awarded her the Meyer Medal for Foreign Plant Importation. Previously it had been given once a year, and ten men had been the recipients. Kate was the first woman so honored. This medal may be seen in the San Diego Historical Society's Research Archives among Kate's letters and diaries. There it reposes in its original plush lined case bearing her name. The story behind the medal is worth telling. Frank Meyer came to the United States from Holland where he had been head gardener under Heys de Vries in Amsterdam. He was noted for his travels to China and for the large number of plants sent from there. After many years of plant exploration in China and Asia, in 1918 he lost his life in the Yangtse River. His will revealed that he had left $1,000 to David Fairchild, Director of the Seed and Plant Production Company with which Meyer had been associated. The will directed Fairchild to use this sum for a holiday for the office workers. But Fairchild (Author of *The World Was My Garden*) and the office staff felt this should be used to establish a medal for plant importation as a memorial to Meyer.

Appropriately, on the night in March of 1939 when the medal was presented to Kate, Fairchild's book was reviewed as the program. The medal was designed by Theodore Spicer-Simson to portray, on the face, the earliest expedition recorded in history for the express purpose of introducing useful plants from one country to another. Queen Hatshepsut of the eighteenth dynasty of Egyptian civilization, about 1570 B.C., is shown together with the loading of incense trees she was bringing from the Land of Punt to her palace in Thebes. The theme was taken from a bas-relief she had executed on one of her palace walls. The trees are being carried up the gangplank to the deck of the Queen's ahahbijeh (ship) preparatory to sailing for Alexandria.

On the reverse side of the medal in Chinese letters is the poem of Chik'and, a poet of the Tong Dynasty, 618 A.D. "In the glorious luxuriance of the hundred plants, he takes delight.'' On either side of this inscription are cones of the white barked pine and the tsao or jujube tree of China, two plant importations made by Frank N. Meyer into America.

Miss Sessions died March 24, 1940. Her name has been made indelible in San Diego. In Pacific Beach, an elementary school is called, *Kate Sessions,* and on the 100th anniversary of her birth, November 8, 1957, a beautiful park at the end of Lamont Street on Soledad Road was dedicated to her memory. On Balboa Avenue stands the tree planted by her and dedicated as a State Historical Landmark. These are all enduring symbols of a grateful city for her many contributions to its beauty.

Water — An Ever Present Problem

The need for water was a problem in San Diego from earliest times. Many amusing incidents are discovered in searching for the history of the park. For example, in 1890 the city was voting for the organization of a local water system. F.T. McNealey, one of the first attorneys in the city, was then Judge. He declared that the number of votes cast, compared to the number of voters registered, has never been equalled anywhere. He filed a brief stating that the election was illegal, and therefore the issue was void.

In the spring of 1890 the 700 trees planted by the Ladies Annex were suffering for lack of water. A representative of the San Diego Flume (Water) Company sent word that rather than have the trees die he would send water at company expense. A few days later, according to the paper, M.C. Healion of the Flume Company was sending water for the trees. In November, 1890 the *San Diego Union* reported that the ladies' tract in the park was coming on vigorously . . . but north of Kalmia one of the park squares was being used for the pasturage of a burro and a goat.

The Golden Hill Park area in the south east corner of the park became a focal point of interest to the surrounding community in 1889-90. Leroy Wright and Mathias F. Heller were leaders in improving and planting the area. For a long time this was the choice part of the 1,400 acres. Leroy Wright, former state senator, described Golden Hill in the early days: "The first playground in the city park was in the section north of the 25th street entrance. Swings were erected and the ground about was covered with sawdust. Sand was hauled from the beach and piled up for a children's play area. The most in-

Senator Leroy Wright

City Park, looking at
what is today Marston
Point, c. 1900

viting amusement was afforded by an eucalyptus tree which the children called, "Cornuta Lehmenni." Four large limbs had been broken off by being overcrowded with children. This afforded easy access to the tree, and it was not an unusual sight to see the tree filled with children like so many blackbirds."

Mat F. Heller undertook further development of Golden Hill in 1901 and 1902. An Italian gardener was employed. Palm trees and eucalyptus trees were planted. Rose gardens were started. About this time the Golden Hill Company was organized, and several hundred dollars were raised for planting that district. Mr. Heller, with the help of friends, built the first tennis court in the Golden Hill area, started the movement for a nine-hole golf course, and sparked the interest in the north playgrounds.

Julius Wangenheim

On August 15, 1902 Julius Wangenheim suggested to C.C. Frevert, president of the Chamber of Commerce, that a park improvement committee be appointed. Accordingly, Wangenheim was named chairman, with U.S. Grant, Jr., George W. Marston, William Clayton and D.F. Garrettson appointed to serve with him. Frevert also named a special committee on park plans, naming George Marston, Kate Sessions and Ernest White to serve.

Julius Wangenheim was born in San Francisco, graduated from the University of California in 1887, and worked for a time as an engineer for the Southern Pacific Railway. In the meantime he married Laura Klauber, and in the mid-nineties joined the wholesale grocery firm in which his father-in-law, Abraham, and the latter's son Melville were chief owners. The firm became, and still is, the Klauber Wangenheim Company. He was ever identified with civic, cultural and educational matters. He served on many civic boards, among which were the Park Commission and the Library Board. He was President of the Bank of Commerce.

On January 18, 1930 he was elected President of the Fine Arts Society. In 1931 he designed and demonstrated a solar clock which in appearance resembled a brass urn. With George W. Marston and Leroy Wright, Wangenheim founded the San Diego Historical Society on December 13, 1928. The next year, on December 11, he donated a sun dial of his own invention to Balboa Park. It was installed at Sixth and Date Streets, but has long since perished.

On January 18, 1930 Wangenheim was elected president of the Fine Arts Society. He died on March 10, 1942. The Julius Wangenheim Room in the San Diego Public Library, which houses the greater part of his personal library, serves as a perpetual memorial to him.

George White Marston

In time and leadership given Balboa Park, surely George White Marston must be considered to be the greatest of all who furthered the park development. He was born in 1850 in Wisconsin. At the age of fourteen he enrolled in Beloit Academy. As a youth, he worked in a grist mill and in a bank; studied one year at the University of Michigan, and at the age of twenty, went with his father by rail to San Francisco in October of 1870. He came to San Diego to find a better climate, arriving on the old side-wheeler called *The Senator.*

Immediately he took a job at Horton House where one of the duties of the young clerk was to use the feather duster on the grimy, dusty incoming passengers on the Yuma Stagecoach. He described the Horton House as being richly furnished with marble top tables and wash stands. After six months he took a job in a store owned by Aaron Pauly which was located on the water front. In 1872 he worked in a store belonging to J. Nash which, he said, was the cheapest store in the city. A signboard announced "Established 1868. Population then 23." In 1873 Marston and Charles Hamilton bought out Nash; the firm then became Hamilton and Marston. Hamilton was descriptive in his advertising copy, describing their butter as "being as good as one could expect after its long transportation from Poway."

In 1878 on August 8, Marston married Anna Lee Gunn, a teacher at the San Diego Academy.

That same year he opened his own business. His first year's sales were $19,680 — about equal to one day's sales sixty years later. When the boom of 1860 broke, Marston found it necessary to augment his earnings by working part time as a teller in the Consolidated National Bank. His employer told him he was a poor teller, but he would make a good bank president. As business increased, he moved four times. The last location was at Sixth and C streets where "Marston's" was famous for quality of service and merchandise.

In 1872 while still a clerk, Marston along with Charles Hamilton opened a free reading room, the forerunner of today's excellent library. Marston served on the Library Board for many years. He also served as Secretary, then President of the Chamber of Commerce. In 1873 he organized the Benevolent Society of San Diego, prototype of our social agencies. He was active in the Presbyterian Church and in 1886 he helped to organize the Congregational Church. In 1882 a few young men met in his store and started the local Y.M.C.A. He served on the Y.M.C.A. Board until his death, and was President of the Board for twenty-four years.

George White Marston

His great love of the out-of-doors was shown by his contribution in personal time and influence, as well as in financial support to Balboa Park. His love for his city and for the park were exemplified when, as a member of the committee to make plans for the park, he would settle for none but the best and personally financed an expert from New York who made plans.

In 1903 the work of grading, preparing the soil, laying out a water system and planting, was progressing and Mr. Marston as Park Commissioner watched over it.

In July of 1929, on the 160th birthday of San Diego and the anniversary of Fr. Junípero Serra's simple service on Presidio Hill, Marston presented to the city beautiful Presidio Park and the cathedral-like Junípero Serra Museum. Mr. Marston loved the Borrego Desert country and bought hundreds of acres of land in the area. He, with others, was instrumental in the State of California action to create Anza Borrego Desert State Park. When this was accomplished, he gave the land which he owned to the people of the state. Many colleges benefitted from Marston's concern for education; among these were Berkeley's School of Religion, Pomona College, and Claremont Associated Colleges.

Robert Herring, in his "The Education of George Marston," said that any biography of Marston should be called, "The Lives of the Man;" that his education had been mainly living in the thick of things. Marston died on May 31, 1946 at the age of 95.

The Park

Once the Park Improvement Committee was functioning, the Ladies Annex of the Chamber of Commerce offered their help and organized a drive for funds from private donations. In the San Diego Historical Society's Research Archives is one of the forms they used.

San Diego   1902
I/we agree to pay the Park Improvement Committee of the Chamber of Commerce the sum of _____
Dollars when called upon; the sum to be used for improvement of the park near 7th Street and Fir Street, as outlined by your committee.

(Signed)

Members of the Auxiliary were: Kate O. Sessions, Mrs. F.C. Hennessy, Ada Smith, Mrs. J.L. Doyle, Miss A.E. Frost, Mrs. Waldo S. Waterman, Mrs. Alda M. Ferris and Mrs. B.C. Lockwood.

On September 2, 1902, the *San Diego Union* reported the results of the drive:

For Park Improvement Fund

Allyn Bequest	$3,000
George Marston	1,000
S.D. Cuyamaca Eastern R.R.	100
La Jolla, P.B. Railroad	200
Klauber Wangenheim Co.	200
First National Bank	250
Garrettson Investment Company	100
Simon Levi	100
F.R. Burnham	100
U.S. Grant Jr.	250
Capt. W.R. Maize	100
I.N. Lawson	100
Total	$5,500

In the same year the city trustees voted $20,000 for park improvement, and they also appointed a Park Committee.

Mary Coulston another woman, who was destined to make a large contribution to the Park, arrived in San Diego in 1902. She was a friend of Kate Sessions, and had first been assistant, then later the editor of *Garden and Forest* in New York City. This was the oldest garden magazine published. She and Miss Sessions spent much time together. Miss Kate's notes show that almost immediately on her arrival, Kate took her to call on Mrs. Marston, and within minutes the conversation turned to the park. In October of 1902, she was persuaded to become executive Secretary of the Park Improvement Committee.

Mary Coulston was an excellent press writer, an authority on gardens, and, according to George Marston and Kate Sessions, she gave a powerful impetus to park enthusiasm, and wise direction to park committees. Two huge scrapbooks of editorials under her name, and newspaper clippings of the period concerning the park may be seen at the Historical Society's Research Archives. These were a collection which she made for George Marston. In her long and many editorials on the Park she combined a skill in writing with a happy faculty of gentle persuasion. When there was strong opposition to the Park Committee plans, she skirted around proposals of the other side and and invariably supported those who wanted nothing but the best for the Park.

She wrote in a knowledgeable manner that could bring no offense. Beginning in 1902 and running along for the next eight years, almost every issue carried a discussion of park needs, and how the drive for funds was progressing. One paper carried news that a large number of Park Improvement Buttons had been ordered. These would be given to all subscribers regardless of the amount given. One of these is in the files of the Historical Society.

On October 17, 1902 an editorial suggested that San Diego might give a Band Concert to raise funds for the park, and that the owners of the Opera House should be invited to donate the use of the theater for this worthy purpose. The following October, a concert and operetta were given by the Amphion Club at the Isis Theater — and earned $300 for the Park Fund.

Meanwhile a search was under way for the best available person to plan the development of the park. Mrs. Coulston wrote letters to many prominent leaders asking about this. Among others she sought advice from Mrs. Leland Stanford, Benjamin Ide Wheeler, president of the University of California, and Mrs. Phoebe Hearst. Having been active in garden groups in New York City, Mrs. Coulston knew the Samuel V. Parsons firm there. John McLaren, Superintendent of the Golden Gate Park in San Francisco also recommended this firm. Parsons was President of the American Society of Landscape Architects and was Consulting Architect for greater New York.

News was circulated that an eastern firm might be employed to make plans for the park. The Sunday paper of October 3 carried an editorial from a reader which said: "A San Diego landscape artist, fully qualified and familiar with the shrubs and soil, will not plant an oak where only pines will grow." And the San Diego *Sun* of the same date carried comments that expressed concern about bringing in outsiders to plan the park. "We had outsiders to plan our library. Wasn't that enough? What should have been our beautiful library building is more suggestive of an eastern jail. Let us not turn our park, robbed of all its natural features, into a model of an eastern cemetery."

Mary B. Coulston replied to these criticisms in her gentle, skillful manner. She wrote: "The best qualified landscape architect who can make a plan assuring the most picturesque landscape should be employed, whether he comes from the east or the west. And the best California authority on plants and planting suitable for San Diego should be called in to work jointly with the designer of the landscape."

Another of Mrs. Coulston's editorials states: "Making the plan belongs in the department of land architecture; and developing the realization of that plan comes within the scope of landscape gardening." How well she spoke for today when she wrote: "The unusual interest of the park authorities, all busy men with large interests of their own, indicates the wide importance of a park in San Diego, and this attraction will be, not alone to San Diego, but to persons actively interested in plants and beautiful landscape effects in other parts of the world, and to a large number of tourists and visitors to whom the park will be a special attraction."

On October 8, the paper reported that George Marston had gone east on a business trip and that while he was away, he would probably look for a landscape architect to make plans for the park. A week later Marston sent word from New York that he, personally, would take care of all expenses of the park plans (estimated at from $10,000 to $15,000), and therefore all contributions made to the Park Improvement Committee could be used to develop the park. (In addition to paying for the park plans, his records disclosed that he had deposited to the Park Fund at various times, $20,982.14 and that only $23.45 had been refunded to him.)

Meanwhile the Ladies Annex were busily engaged in creating general interest in park improvement; they solicited and received subscriptions from lodges and organizations, in addition to many personal donations.

On October 20, Marston wired that he had engaged Samuel Parsons to make plans for the improvement and beautification of the park. In Marston's *History of the City Parks* is an account of Parsons' arrival at San Diego on December 21, 1902, and of his reaction after looking over the site. "The setting of the park between a vast mountain system on the one hand and the broad ocean on the other is unique. Harbor, bay, islands, sea, promontories, mountains, and miles of open country — each with its own unusual and distinct characteristics, are all incorporated in the park scheme, form an inseparable and a vital part of it; hundreds of square miles of land and sea are thereby added to the territory of the park."

The New York *Evening Post* noted Parsons' work out in San Diego by printing his description of the Park: "The Park is nearly square. It is one and one-half miles across. The skyline to the north is outlined by chains of mountains 10,000 feet high; the San Jacinto range is eighty miles away from north to north east. To the southwest, the Coronado Islands are weird, fantastic forms in the unlimited space of ocean. To the northwest is Point Loma, a long peninsula of elevation of several hundred feet. Beyond are glimpses of the Pacific, and below the beautiful San Diego Bay covering twenty-two square miles, in this wonderful land."

The year 1903 was pioneer year for the park. On January 1, 1903 funds totalling $10,282 had been subscribed for park improvement. Of this, $1,252.70 had been raised by the Ladies Annex. The first six months after Parsons arrived, were devoted to surveys, contour maps, working plans and much preliminary activity. A pattern, established at this time, has prevailed throughout the city's history. Non-official agencies and funds were used together with city funds and workers in order to accomplish a purpose. The city had appointed a committee which functioned through the city public works department, and this group worked shoulder to shoulder with the Park Improvement Committee which was appointed by the Chamber of Commerce. To illustrate:

In January 1903 Mayor Frary asked the City Council to authorize a survey of the park. The original ordinance enabling the survey was passed on April 29 and is reproduced here:

San Diego, California: Be it ordained by the Common Council of San Diego as follows:

Section one: The City Engineer of the City of San Diego be and is hereby authorized and directed to do and perform whatever surveying that he may be requested to do and perform by the Public Works of said city; in the improvement of the 1400 acre park in said city providing that such surveying shall not require the employment of any additional men which have not been authorized by this common council in writing and provided the expense shall not exceed the sum of $10. (ten dollars).

Section two: This ordinance shall take effect and be in force from and after its passage and approval.

Passed and adopted on April 29, 1903. M.J. Perrin, President, Board of Aldermen, City of San Diego. Approved April 30, 1903 — Frank P. Frary, Mayor of San Diego.

The auditor's certificate is in the museum also:

Certified that the appropriation made of indebtedness incurred by reason of the provision of the annexed ordinance in regard to surveying in City Park can be made or incurred without the violation of any of the provisions of the charter of the City of San Diego, California. April 29, 1903.

The expense of the survey was met in this way. City Engineer d'Hemecourt secured from the Los Angeles firm, Lippincott's U.S. Geological Staff, their Chief Engineer, Lee M. Hyde, to work for the Park Improvement Committee and to be paid by that group the sum of $7.00 per day. This was necessary since the city did not allow for any funds excepting for public works employees already on the payroll at $3.50 per day, and only voters and property owners could qualify for city employment. Hyde could not qualify for city pay; therefore, he was paid by the Park Improvement Fund.

One man, Alverson, foreman of the survey group, asked $4.50 per day; the city could pay only $3.50. George W. Marston arranged with Engineer d'Hemecourt to allow Marston to pay the extra dollar. Hyde was assigned to survey only three-fourth's of the park. The project was to take four men forty days to finish. This is a typical example of how private donations dovetailed with city funds to develop the park.

Beginning in April 1903, the Park Improvement Committee met every week. Kate Sessions was selected by the committee to arrange for irrigation of the west side of the park. She approached Joseph Flint, head of the Water Department and the result was another City Ordinance, interesting reading in the light of costs years later.

The Public Works to purchase:
286 linear feet 4" cast iron pipe
1681 linear feet 3" cast iron pipe
2710 linear feet 2" cast iron pipe
2440 linear feet 1" cast iron pipe
Directed to lay, under the Superintendent of the Water Department according to the plan furnished by the Board of Public Works. The total expense not to exceed $1,715.21.

Part of this strict economy of the city toward the park may have been due to the $500,000 bond issue already before the voters. The Park Improvement Committee deemed it unwise to ask for more tax funds at this time. However, John MacLean, formerly the foreman of Golden Gate Park, was employed as head gardener at $60.00 per month to work under the direction of Mary Coulston, executive secretary of the Park Improvement Committee. One of MacLean's first duties was to stop the shooting of mocking birds and meadow larks in the park.

The Park Improvement Committee sought an inexpensive fertilizer and mulch to be used for park planting. Mr. C.C. Frevert contacted Mr. Hackett of the Street Department, and also Mr. Meyers, Chairman of the City Council Street Committee, regarding the procurement of street sweepings; also manure from the city barns of the Fire Department, Public Works Department and Street Department. The street department had sold such at $2.00 per load and averaged eight to ten loads per month. Mr. Frevert was able to obtain this fertilizer from the City Department for the park at no cost.

From this time on, interest in the park increased. The San Diego Commercial College offered free clerical and typing assistance from the students. On March 15, the Golden Hill Civic Club, which had sponsored the development of that section of the park, asked George Marston to address their meeting at Twenty-Fourth and H Streets. He paid tribute to the spirit and work of the group and told of Mr. Parsons' developments in the park. He asked the Golden Hill group to continue to take the lead in that area for another year; then the Park Committee would take charge of it, along with the rest of the park. In May, 1903, John McLaren, Superintendent of Golden Gate Park, sent a gift of plants from San Francisco as a gesture of interest and friendship on behalf of the new park.

From early spring of 1903, the Park Improvement Secretary's notes disclose meetings with representatives of the Woodmen and Foresters, fraternal groups which were interested in arranging for a tree-planting in the park. At first they suggested 1,000 trees. But that number seemed impractical and Parsons suggested 150 and 350 of two varieties of eucalyptus trees. Kate Sessions suggested that these come from the 300 per year that she had agreed to furnish the city. The lodges were to pay for the trees; however the lodge groups and the Park Improvement Committee shared differing concepts of what this amount would be, and the Park Committee, it turned out, shouldered the hard work and received about one third of what they expected toward the project. The date finally set for the planting was July 4. The planting area was at Tenth and Ash Streets.

The Park Committee while wishing to co-operate with any interest in park development, saw obstacles in the plan. Children ran rampant in the area and might injure the young trees; cows were allowed to pasture here; at least fifty were tethered in the park, and a large herd roamed in Pound (Cabrillo) Canyon. However, preparations were made for the planting.

All of the hard work was done by the Park Committee. One man worked for a week pulling out the tall weeds; three boys worked a day picking up tin cans, and four men worked ten days digging 500 holes; of these, twenty-five needed blasting. Mary Coulston and T.S. Brandegee had gone out previously and staked out the location for the trees. After the holes were dug, they were filled with mulch and street sweepings. Lastly, on the day before the planting, each hole was given a barrel of water. This had to be hauled in barrels on a water cart from some distance, so that four horses were needed with two extra to alternate with the four. The pull over the rough terrain was a hard load for the beasts. The water was fed to the holes by means of a fifty foot hose. When fifty holes were yet to be watered an axle on the cart broke. Judge Luce came to the rescue and offered a water cart from his property. Next, on this day before the planting, they placed 400 young trees in the watered holes. Early the following morning the gardeners put the remainder in place. Printed instructions were given

Date Street looking toward the park, 1906

the lodge representative stating that all that was needed now was for the lodge members to press the earth about each tree, and that they could use their feet for this simple task. The lodge group had asked for the removal of shrubbery at the place of the speakers' platform, but the Park Committee forbid this destruction, and the stand was placed amidst chaparral and other growth.

On the 4th of July, 1903, a special train from Los Angeles brought 500 excursionists to San Diego. A great parade was held with a band in the lead. However, long before the parade was over, the hour for the speaker had arrived. The newspaper reported that exactly 155 men, women, children and jack-rabbits heard W.W. Bowers, former Congressman and now State Senator, make the address of the day. Nevertheless, it was no disrespect to speaker Bowers that the crowd was of such small dimension; "It was doubtful if Grover Cleveland or Booker T. Washington could have drawn a respectable audience in the wilds of San Diego Park that afternoon."

After the parade, Mrs. Coulston and Mr. Brandegee again went to the planting area. Several hundred flags had been dispersed throughout the grounds. About noon two Foresters and Mr. Magley, head of the lodge arrangements, appeared and planted a sugar gum tree which had been sent the day before. As the men left, Mr. Magley reported that this finished the lodge participation in the planting. The trees were sufficiently protected, and on the following Monday they were given necessary care, tied to stakes, and watered on successive days.

In July of 1903, George Cooke of Parsons' firm arrived, and actual construction began at Sixth and Date Streets. Up to this time the park had been used as a dumping ground, and it was littered with old barbed wire, baling wire, tin cans, barrel staves and refuse such as a city of fifteen to twenty thousand would dispose of. In addition, contractors had helped themselves to land in the southwest corner. They used this, in part, to fill the canyon on Fifth Street. As a result of this excavation, the area presented the appearance of having been opened up by some hydraulic mining company. No 1,400 acres, from the Colorado River to the Bay, could have presented a less attractive sight when work was begun.

Park operations commenced with blasting, hard-pan shooting, digging, shoveling and grading with men and mules in a revelry of sweat and dirt. Marston and his friends were there, constantly watching the work. Some would say, "Marston, you'd better give this up. It's a natural home for cactus, coyotes and jack rabbits. It ain't no park and never will be." Marston

would reply. "A greater prophet in Israel has said, 'The desert shall blossom as a rose.'" Marston said there were about as many landscape artists as there have been lay engineers. Among the plans proposed was a dam across Cabrillo Canyon (Pound Canyon then.) There should be one across Switzer Canyon also. Two beautiful lakes would be made in the park. Sun fish and gold fish would be visible from the banks which would hang with green flowering shrubs and vines. Water lilies would float on the lakes, white swans and many kinds of ducks would adorn them. But Parsons vetoed the lakes. There was not sufficient rainfall; the lakes would be mud lakes with stench arising from them as life in the lakes would die.

John McLean began work on a lathhouse located at the park nursery; meanwhile seeds and trees were being selected. The College of Forestry at Santa Monica (University of California) sent a large number of seeds of various trees. The general plan of planting was to be the use of palms and other trees with a moderate need of water, and arranged in harmonious grouping as to foliage and color scheme, and with special care taken to preserve fine views. This could be done by limiting the height of plantings at strategic points.

In the area south of the War Memorial Building and north of the Natural History Museum, in the early 1900s some golf enthusiasts had established a golf course. Much of it was a dirt course; in wet weather weeds and alfalfa covered the grounds. The members tried cutting the course with scythes which proved very strenuous. They looked for an easy way out, and obtained the sheep from Charles Hardy's pens to eat the greens. However, the watchful poundmaster discovered that the sheep were there, and impounded them. After much scurrying about between the club members, Mayor, Councilmen and Poundmaster, the sheep were finally allowed to finish the grass and return to Hardy's pens.

On August 27, 1903, Cooke returned to New York saying that the park was well under way and that, upon his return in January, he would push planting from Date to Upas Streets, including the west canyon. On December 19, in readiness for Cooke's return, trees and shrubs were on hand and more would be obtained from Los Angeles, Pasadena and Santa Barbara nurseries. Cooke returned December 21 and was well pleased with all that had been done, especially with all of the available plantings for the park for use immediately on the finish of grading. These were under the care of E. Barnard and had been obtained from nurseries in San Francisco, Santa Barbara and San Diego. Many trees and plants had been started in the park nurseries. Mr. Cooke spent Christmas with Mr. Brandegee. They selected a favorable place for a palm canyon, a side canyon leading down from Pound Canyon and up to a grove of Monterey pines in the Howard Tract.

Early in 1904 a squabble arose when a change of plans placed an entrance to the park from Kalmia instead of Juniper, as originally planned. Also, the west road was changed to go through Kate Sessions' nursery, instead of the original site. "No matter what plans are adopted, they cannot please everyone," said Mr. Frevert, "but the plans we hope to adopt, we think will please the great majority of citizens." (the *San Diego Union* had a library file marked "Park Squabbles.") Opponents would have obliterated Balboa Park Drive and would have made an outer boulevard along Sixth Avenue, 150 feet wide for five blocks on the west side. A spokesman for the Park Committee said, "They propose to incorporate as part of the park system, a highway utterly incongruous with the plans for the park. It would be an even, unbroken surface, 150 feet wide, and one that might be as consistently introduced as to introduce a wash tub on a banquet table." The Federation of City Clubs responded to an urgent call for a meeting, on February 14, 1904. They supported Parsons' plans and asked that they be pushed forward. Signers, as Presidents were: Melville Klauber, Horton Improvement Club; C.C. Hackleman, Central Improvement Club; J.A. Young, La Jolla, and Naylor Newkirk, Florence Hill and University Heights Improvement Clubs.

On January 19, news divulged another controversy. A local company had offered free oil for the park roadways when they were graded and ready. When work was stopped between Date and Fir Streets because of the hassle over the wide boulevard the offer to furnish oil was withdrawn. A tense situation developed. Finally on February 8, the Balboa Park Drive (then called the west road) quarrel was resolved; the affair returned to the original status; the offer was renewed and the donor of the oil extended until May the deadline for its use. This was done in order to give time for the preparation of the road beds. John H. Day was the dealer who donated the oil and who had made the offer through the Chamber of Commerce. The local paper gave a timely, and for all time, admonition, "We ought all to work together, and if we do, we can make San Diego the most attractive place in the world."

An article in the *Union* for January 30, 1904 described the difficulty of ground preparation in the park. "Hard pan makes hard work." All plows and scrapers were working on the land which had been occupied by Miss Sessions'

nursery opposite Redwood Street. Here the ground was of loam and sand. But in from Laurel Street were seven or eight men engaged in drilling holes in hard pan which had broken three plows in a distance of twenty yards. Dynamite charges were placed in the holes, and an electric spark set them off. Between Nutmeg and Maple Streets were laid a connected system of wires setting off any number of charges simultaneously.

An area of the park, now mostly occupied by the Naval Hospital, was called the Howard Tract in honor of Bryant Howard who planted the first of any trees in the park. Some have said he should be called the father of Balboa Park. When one of his relatives complained that some of those trees had been uprooted, Marston explained that they were not fine trees. For months they had been trimmed by a broom manufacturer until some of them looked more like spooks than trees. After the roads were completed in this area, eucalyptus trees would be planted which would improve the tract by affording a broad street and a truer perspective. (This area was located along Park Boulevard as far south as Russ Street.)

Opposition kept raising its ugly head. Owners of the property adjacent to the park wished the plans changed for their special benefit. The *San Diego Union* expressed exasperation, "How can there be trouble with the Park improvement within the park when the park is for all of the people. Property owners, interested in their own property, have no more jurisdiction in the park than if they lived in Logan Heights or Middletown."

Melville Klauber

The elimination of the horse from the streets has done much toward our speed of living. In February of 1905 the horse was king of the highway. We read, "Police Chief Thomas gives fair notice to all drivers of power vehicles that City ordinance regulated speed and would be enforced. Between the boundaries of B and K Streets and 3rd and 7th Streets, the speed may not exceed six miles per hour, and at all street crossings it must be reduced to four miles per hour. Automobile drivers must remember that horses have the right of prior occupancy on the highway. Drivers of traction engines must give way. Automobiles with rubber tires come so noiselessly on a pedestrian before he is aware, that he has no time to escape."

On March 3, 1905, Cooke was called back to New York. He stated that he would not return in his official capacity; the work was in such shape that it would advance with no further trouble or delays.

An Arbor Day Celebration

Professor Davidson, Superintendent of Schools, wanted to interest the children in nature study, plant life, and to create civic interests on the part of his students. The Ladies Annex suggested a contribution from the children to the Park Improvement Fund. But the Board of Education did not wish the children to be asked for money. Rather, it was suggested, let the children prepare seedling trees under the direction of the Park Committee, for use in the park.

As an Arbor Day celebration on March 17, 1904, several of the schools decided to have a tree planting in the park. Before he left for the east, architect Cooke selected two points on the west hillside of Pound (Cabrillo) Canyon, on a line east of Palm and Quince Streets as tree sites. He suggested that on one, they could plant Monterey Cypress and on the other, Monterey Pines. The points would be called Cypress Point and Pine Point. About sixty trees were to be planted. The schools participating were Russ High School (San Diego High School), B Street School, Middletown, Sherman Heights, East, Fifth Ward, University Heights and H Street. Promptly at ten o'clock on the seventeenth of March, the pupils assembled and marched to the park for the exercises. Trees were marked with the name of each participating school.

The Russ High School orchestra accompanied the children as they sang, "Flower of Liberty," "America," and "My Own Native Land." Superintendent Davidson made an efficient music director as the children stood massed under the banners of their own schools. The President of the Board of Education, George W.

Marston, spoke. Mrs. Coulston read a telegram from President Theodore Roosevelt which said:

"Hearty Greetings and congratulations on the establishment of Arbor Day! Your love of trees now will make you, as men and women, lovers of forests both for their natural beauty and economic value. Let your motto be to preserve and care for these as a permanent function for the production of food, as storage place for water which is needed for irrigation, and playgrounds for young and old."
(Signed) Theodore Roosevelt

The telegram was addressed to "The School Children of San Diego, Room 7, Sefton Building, San Diego, California, care of The Park Improvement Committee." Next she read a telegram from Governor George Pardee:

"I am glad to know that you are going to spend the day in the noble occupation of planting trees. You could not do a better thing for your city, for yourselves and for those who come after you. The trees will live as long as you do and longer, and every year they will make San Diego more beautiful and inviting. I hope that every child will take part in the good work."
(Signed) George Pardee, Governor

The Russ student body President, Frank Johnson spoke. He said:

"It is appropriate, at the dawn of a new era in the history of our city that we, who must soon be guardians of this park should have the privilege of taking an active part today in the planting, and we can but hope that these exercises will inspire us with a higher sense of the duties and responsibilities of the citizen which we must assume in the future."

In closing, he led a cheer for Mr. Marston, and for his leadership and devotion to the park. Over 4,000 persons attended the Arbor Day Celebration.

Frank P. Davidson had been named Superintendent of Schools in 1890. He was a graduate of Wittenberg College, Ohio. In 1904 members of the school board tried to fire him. At the next election, the citizens retired those members opposing him and elected new members favorable to Davidson. A suit to fire him was taken first to the appellate court, then to the Supreme Court. It was known as the Davidson vs. Baldwin Case. The decision upheld Davidson and stated that a superintendent cannot be dismissed during his term without just cause.

A recent visit to the area of that first Arbor Day observance showed a fine growth of cypress trees and pine trees which must have been little saplings on April 17, 1904.

The death of Mary Coulston was announced on October 11, 1904. In Kate Sessions' notes she stated that according to the request of the deceased, she was cremated and her ashes were buried under a Cedar of Lebanon tree in the park.

A Look At Politics

Records show that in the national election of 1904, San Diego cast 2,382 votes for Republican Theodore Roosevelt, 768 votes for Socialist Eugene Debbs and 666 votes for the Democratic candidate Alton Brooks Parker. In 1905 there was a revolt against what was called, "Boss Rule" in San Diego. This resulted in the adoption of a city charter which reduced the City Council from twenty-seven to nine members. In the 1905 city election Captain John L. Sehon, a retired army officer, was nominated for mayor by the Independents. He had the support of some Democrats and of some Republicans, the latter being known as Progressives. The campaign was exceedingly bitter. Sehon won the election. The Republicans filed suit to find if a retired army officer could hold public office. Sehon evaded the filing of legal papers, and at 2:00 a.m. of the day he was to assume office, he forced the front doors of the City Hall at Fifth and G Streets; broke a door to gain entrance to the mayor's office, and took possession. He defied his opponents on the grounds that "possession is nine tenths of the law," and although the case was taken to the Supreme Court, he held his office.

In 1905 the City voted to support the park with a tax levy by an amendment to the City Charter. Not less than five cents or more than eight cents per $100.00 dollar valuation was voted to be spent by the Park Commissioners. On April 17 the first Park Commission was appointed. The members were: George W. Marston, President, Ernest E. White, Secretary, and A. Moran. From 1903 to 1910 the roadways were built and named. A partial water system was installed; the west side was planted from Upas to Date Streets; Golden Hill was further developed. In addition to the natural difficulties, there was constant opposition from the minority, a shortage of water, and a popular impatience that trees would not grow with more speed. But still, it was a brave beginning for a great park.

In 1905 the country was experiencing a boom. With work started on the Panama Canal, San Diego could envision a new role as the first port of call on the Pacific Coast and an end to her long isolation.

City Park Arbor Day, 1904

The city of San Diego and, in the background, newly named Balboa Park, c. 1910

At Last The Park Is Named

In 1910 the park began to look much as it does now. Until that year it had no name, save Park or City Park. In order to find a suitable name, a contest was held. Names suggested were Horton, Silvergate, Pacific and Darien. The winner was Mrs. Harriet Phillips, a member of the Pioneer Society and of the San Diego Club, with her sug-gestion of Balboa. The name was to honor the Spanish explorer, Vasco Núñez de Balboa, who first saw the Pacific Ocean from the Gulf of Uraba when he climbed the summit of a range of mountains near Darien in Central America. On October 10, 1910, the name Balboa Park was officially adopted by the Park Commissioners, Thomas O'Halloran, Moses A. Wallace and Leroy A. Wright.

THE PANAMA—CALIFORNIA EXPOSITION

On July 9, 1909 G. Aubrey Davidson, presiding as president of the Chamber of Commerce, said that inasmuch as the Panama Canal would be completed in 1915, and San Diego would be the first port of call north of the canal, the city should stage an exposition to celebrate this event. Davidson, president also of the Southern Trust and Savings Bank, was one of the great boosters of San Diego.

Davidson said further that San Diego had a beautiful bay, and that nothing was being done with it: that such an undertaking as an exposition would provide buildings for Balboa Park, and that it would bolster the sagging economy. Although the action of the voters had been discouraging a few years earlier when they had voted down bonds intended to improve the west side of the park, still something had to be done to put San Diego on the map and to advertise it to the rest of the world. The Chamber of Commerce agreed wholeheartedly with this suggestion. Davidson then appointed a committee to organize the exposition. Thus, on September 3, 1909 The Panama-California Exposition was duly organized with this board of directors: L.A. Blochman, George Burnham, William Clayton, D.C. Collier, G. Aubrey Davidson, Lyman J. Gage, D.F. Garrettson, John H. Gay, Ralph Granger, U.S. Grant, Jr., C.E. Grosbeck, F.W. Jackson, Fred Jewell, Simon Levi, L.S. McClure, Arthur H. Marston, J.F. Sefton Jr., A.G. Spalding, John D. Spreckels, Julius Wangenheim and C.I. Williams. Articles of Incorporation were formulated and sent to the Secretary of State in Sacramento. Plans were made to raise funds needed for this gigantic enterprise.

On September 10, 1909 the board of directors selected the officers of the Panama-California Exposition Company: president, Ulysses S. Grant; first vice-president, John D. Spreckels; second vice-president, A.G. Spalding; third vice-president, L.S. McClure; fourth vice-president, G. Aubrey Davidson.

Colonel D.C. Collier

For the man to take charge of the exposition the committee turned to one who had been called San Diego's greatest asset, Colonel D.C. Collier. (The "Colonel" was an honorary title bestowed by some California governor.) Collier was a dynamo as he stepped into this enormous responsibility; he was equal to the occasion. He chose Balboa Park as the location, suggested the type of architecture and established the theme of the exposition as showing the progress of the human race. A noted booster of San Diego, he gave unstinted use of his time and monetary resources to promote the fair. He lobbied in Sacramento and in Washington D.C., at his own expense. At the outbreak of World War I he suggested the loan of the exposition buildings to the navy: thus the beginning of our city as a "navy" town. He supported aviation and organized the Aero Club which brought Glenn Curtiss and the first "flying school" to San Diego. He fathered the transfer of tidelands from state to city thus setting the stage for waterfront and harbor development. He loved beauty, promoted parks in county and city and today we have Collier Parks in San Diego, La Mesa and Ramona, all given by D.C. Collier. He owned the first automobile in the city. Ever wearing a soft broad brimmed hat, a soft shirt (never suspenders) a ready smile, he made an outstanding appearance.

For his part in the San Diego exposition Collier received national recognition and represented the United States in the Centennial Exposition in Brazil in 1922; was chosen director-general for the Sesqui-Centennial in Philadelphia in 1926; and his suggestion — "Century of Progress" — gave the theme to the 1933 Chicago World's Fair.

San Diego's debt to Collier is remembered in Balboa Park on the west wall of the Plaza de California. There a bas-relief shows Collier as he signed his name, "Yours for California." Beneath the signature he is described: David

Colonel D.C. Collier

Charles Collier — A Man of Vision — A Dynamic Leader — A Developer and a Builder — A great and Lovable Character. — The Creative Genius of the Panama-California Exposition — An Inspiration to the Citizens of Today.

San Diego Encounters A Rival — San Francisco

On the same day, September 3, 1909, that San Diego leaders met, incorporated the exposition, and sent notice of this to the state government, a bombshell to these plans was dropped at a meeting in Los Angeles. James McNab, president of the San Francisco Chamber of Commerce announced that San Francisco would hold the official exposition to celebrate the Panama Canal. It would be called the Panama Pacific Exposition and would be held at the same time as that of San Diego. Moreover, San Francisco sent word to San Diego that plans for a fair in San Diego would now be economic suicide.

About this time, New Orleans, aware of the feeling existing between the two California cities tried to promote an exposition. At this, San Diego temporarily withdrew her exposition plans to rise to the defense of San Francisco. During the early part of 1910 there was uncertainty on the part of the local fair directors. While San Diego hesitated and conferred, San Francisco began construction of her fair along the same old lines as past expositions. San Diego leaders conceded their fair would be smaller than at first visualized, but it would be new and different and unlike any other exposition. Meanwhile fair leaders received great encouragement when on February 24, 1910 John D. Spreckels subscribed $100,000 to the exposition and by March 15, 1910 a million dollars had been promised.

Finally on May 7 a mass meeting was held in Lincoln School to decide what to do about holding an exposition. Here such spontaneous enthusiasm was expressed that from that time there was no turning back. At this time it was decided to ask the people to support a bond issue of a million dollars for park improvement and at the election on August 9th the bond issue carried, seven to one.

The 1910 U.S. Census gave San Diego a population of 35,378; San Diego County 61,655; San Francisco 416,000 and Los Angeles 319,918. During the boom of the eighties San Diego had an even greater population; then it had declined to as little at 17,000. But with the census figure of 1910, showing less than 40,000, San Diego would be the smallest city in history to undertake a world fair.

Much resentment was expressed in San Diego, especially when the federal government sanctioned the move by San Francisco to hold a rival fair by inviting the Latin American countries to participate in that exposition.

Apparently at that time there was political chicanery afoot. At present, because of population drift political power is strongest in Southern California — in 1910 the situation was reversed. The Republican party was split by Theodore Roosevelt's Progressive (Bull Moose) Party leaving the main body, the old guard (Stand Patters) under President Taft. San Francisco, it was alleged, promised to deliver California to Taft in the coming election in exchange for bestowing federal favors and official sanction to a Panama Canal celebration in San Francisco.

When President Taft asked the countries to the south to exhibit only in San Francisco it was too much for Joseph W. Sefton, Jr., who in exasperation called the northern city a "Judas." Sefton said that although San Diego announced first, she was willing to give San Francisco the honor for representing California to the world, but by taking away from San Diego the Latin American exhibits our city was given a knife in the back.

In the primary election of August 1912 Samuel C. Evans of Riverside defeated Republican candidate Lewis Kirby of San Diego at this, the local Republicans rallied behind the popular William Kettner, member of the Chamber of Congress and owner of an insurance agency.

Promoters of the exposition were delighted when in November, Taft was defeated in California. Progressives and Republicans combined their slate for the election and Taft's name did not appear on the state ballot. The state as a whole voted for Roosevelt. San Diego county voted for Wilson. San Francisco did not return the state to Taft as had been promised. William Kettner was elected to Congress. On May 23, 1913 President Woodrow Wilson signed a bill to permit free admission of exhibits to the San Diego exposition.

Influenced by the beauty and charm of early Spanish and Mexican settlers, and by the beauty of architecture in Mexico, the fair leaders decided to use for the Panama California Exposition what had come to be called Spanish Colonial architecture.

Spanish Colonial Architecture

In the middle of the eighteenth century, Spain became alarmed over reports that foreign interests were encroaching on her claims in this southwest area; and the King decided to begin colonization, using the church as the basis for this project. Fr. Junípero Serra received his training as a Franciscan priest in Majorca, an island near Spain. A picture of the monastery where he studied reflects the arcades and archways of the buildings left today from the Panama-California Exposition. Fr. Serra was fifty-six years of age when he was sent with soldiers to begin the work of establishing missions in California. He received a foot injury before starting, from which he never fully recovered. He arrived in what is now San Diego on July 1, 1769. On the sixteenth of July he raised a cross and established the first mission in California, and thereby gave San Diego her birthdate.

The Spanish Colonial style of Balboa Park is really a product of the Spanish Renaissance which dates from the expulsion of the Moors about the time Columbus was sailing toward America. To this time little had been written about architecture, and while Spain was controlled by the Moors, artists had not flourished there. After Spain was freed, artists came from France, Italy, Greece and the Orient. The Italians were the first to arrive, and the early buildings were of Italian style. Spain suddenly became wealthy, partly by escaping from the domination of the Moors and partly by wealth brought from the New World. People with no developed taste yearned for the display of wealth, the impression of costliness.

As Spain grew in wealth, taste improved and education advanced. During the seventeenth century, styles of baroque and rococo were borrowed from every school of architecture, and buildings were done in a characteristic florid manner as the artist and patron saw fit. Then came Churrigueresque, named for architect Churriguera who, with his sons had done much to crystalize the dominant features of what was becoming the nearest thing to a standard. Eventually venturesome soldiers who had prospered in New Spain, returned to the mother country. As today, immigrants to America seldom return to their native land and find contentment, so in those days, the soldiers, in spite of their wealth attained in New Spain, failed to gain social recognition. Because of this they became disillusioned and returned to New Spain, bringing with them ideas of architecture. Later Viceroys brought over architects, and the Indians made good carpenters and stone masons.

Many buildings in Mexico were done by men who had only a passing acquaintance with Spanish architecture, and its ornate character. Thus the buildings showed a decided Indian influence.

Warren Baxter wrote that the name "Spanish Colonial" was especially appropriate because the name represents a transfer of architectural forms and traditions from the mother country to the soil of the colony, and the expansion of those forms under auspices which on the material side, were quite as favorable as they were at home. Yet the forms differ from those of the mother country by separation from source and by interpretation by the aboriginal race — the Indians. Hence, the Spanish influence prevailed at the exposition, even to names of features and accessories. During the exposition, Howard Hill was the only English name left in the park.

A Great Event Of Groundbreaking

At last groundbreaking for the exposition was ready to be started. On the 19th of July, 1911, and for the next three days following, the people of San Diego and thousands of visitors from California and from over the world, saw pageantry by day and by night. They relived Old Spain, and spent carefree and pleasure loving hours enjoying California music. The groundbreaking was geared to the founding of San Diego. It began with a military mass by Franciscan Fathers in the southwest part of the park. It was an entrancing color spectacle, seen by 25,000 persons. Priests from northern missions attended. The altar was a replica of an old one at Loreto, B.C. The background was an immense painting of our Lady of Carmel. Franciscan priests had full charge of the event. Celebrant Fr. Benedick, Provincial of the Order, came from St. Louis for the occasion. The Rt. Reverend Thomas James Donaty, Bishop of Los Angeles and Monterey, occupied a purple throne. He was attended by one hundred clergymen. In the sanctuary were the Honorable John Barrett, representing the President of the United States, and Joseph Sefton, representing the Director General of the Exposition. After the military buglers played "Nearer My God to Thee," the Bishop made an historical address as befitted the occasion.

The afternoon program was held at the site of the future exposition buildings. After introductory remarks by U.S. Grant, Jr., there was an invocation by Reverend E.F. Hallenbeck of the Presbyterian Church, and a triple quartet sang the "Exposition Ode."

Joseph W. Sefton, Jr. gave the welcoming speech. Lee C. Gates, representing Governor Johnson spoke, followed by the Honorable John Barrett speaking for President Taft. Sefton next loosened the earth with a silver pick and handed a silver spade to Mr. Barrett who turned the first sod. He passed the spade to the seven dignitaries in attendance, each turning some sod. The spade was returned to Mr. Sefton who turned the last sod. Mr. Barrett made a short speech, and the

*Groundbreaking for the
1915 exposition, July, 1911*

*Exposition groundbreaking
Queen and her court*

flag was unfurled while the band played the National Anthem. Then President Taft pressed a button in Washington, D.C., and the President's flag was unfurled. The flags of all of the southern Republics were unfurled then, and the band played a medley of the national airs of these Nations. Next G. Aubrey Davidson spoke on the imagery of the Panama-California Exposition. Charles C. Moore of San Francisco, spoke on the Panama-Pacific International Exposition of that city.

In the evening, "King Cabrillo" arrived and was escorted to the courthouse where "Queen Ramona" sat on a golden throne. Cabrillo was invited to crown her. The events of the first day ended at the "Isthmus," where there was much merrymaking and noise.

The afternoon of the second day was devoted to a floral parade. That night the program was an historical pageant written by Edwin F. Clough. Henry Kabierske planned the portrayal, and these were the scenes played:

1. The Aztec Priests' Sacrifice to the God of War
2. Balboa taking possession of the Pacific for the King of Spain
3. The Fall of the Aztec Dynasties and the rise of Christian Rule
4. Cabrillo, sent by Cortez in search of Cibola, found California instead.
5. The caravel of Cabrillo.
6. Fr. Serra planting the cross on the shores of San Diego Bay
7. San Diego Mission
8. Raising the first American Flag at Old Town San Diego.
9. King Neptune presiding at the wedding of the Atlantic and Pacific Oceans.
10. The history of San Diego from the discovery by Cabrillo, the founding of the Missions to the present.

On the third day there was a large and elaborate industrial parade. On the fourth and last day, there was produced, "The Pageant of the Missions," said to have been the finest and the most successful attempt at pageantry in America. There were twenty-one floats, each representing a mission. The beginning was San Diego de Alcalá; the end was Mission San Francisco de Solano. The portrayal was from 1769 to 1822, the distance 700 miles from San Diego to Sonoma Valley. Nearly 1,000 characters were in the procession. There were monks, soldiers, knights, Indians and historical characters associated with the missions and their establishment.

The pageant moved in a slow, solemn procession, creating an atmosphere of silence and reverence. Over 25,000 persons attended this finale of the groundbreaking ceremony.

"How the Exposition would benefit San Diego and California" was discussed by G. Aubrey Davidson in the *Exposition News* in December of 1911.

1. With increased population and building operations necessary to growth
2. Profit from the Exposition began with the groundbreaking ceremony

This caused, directly, an increase in bank clearings for one week of $198,000. "We do not need to wait until 1915 for benefits. The $5,000,000 spent in Balboa Park begins earning money at once. Money is spent at the rate of $1,250,000 per year. This project has resulted in an improved harbor, an extra trolley system, street pavement, new buildings for the city, a new depot of Spanish Colonial design built by the Santa Fe Railroad for the Exposition; thousands of new homes are underway or planned; apartment houses, restaurants and so on are planned. There is a $20,000,000 layout. In the meantime, there is work for every type and trade."

About this time Congress authorized the President to request the Republics of South and Central America to participate in the exposition, and this gave encouragement to the exposition officers.

John Morley

At this crucial period in the park development, John Morley became Superintendent of the park. Upon his retirement, twenty-seven years later, this tribute was paid him:

"John Morley retired from the park January 20 after serving 27 years as head of the Park System. A native of Derbyshire, England, Mr. Morley was the son of a well known gardener. He acquired horticultural training which aided him in landscape gardening, park building and management. He studied horticulture in Boston. In 1905 he became Superintendent of parks in Los Angeles. The City Park System developed notably in five years. Then he resigned because of political changes and came to San Diego in 1911 to aid in the development of Balboa Park.

"Mr. Morley said on one occasion that a prime reason for the effectiveness of the San Diego Park System was that it had been kept free from politics. In Balboa Park Mr. Morley had the opportunity to demonstrate, and most successfully, the selection of proper plant material, and how to grow it in a most inhospitable soil, and under adverse ground conditions. Too, he showed

Exposition construction, June 1, 1913

how to arrange it for effectiveness, and thus he transformed an almost barren and unattractive area into a veritable landscape paradise.''

In writing of the exposition, W. Allen Perry said that three men most responsible for the exposition lay-out were Bertram Goodhue, Frank Allen the Engineer, and John Morley, Park Superintendent.

On December 17, 1939, an oak tree was planted in front of the new Balboa Park Club to honor John Morley. Mrs. Mary Greer, President of the San Diego Floral Association, spoke of the long standing desire to honor Mr. Morley, George Marston spoke of the significance of the oak tree to the English people; of its renown with poets, and that the tree would commemorate the work of Mr. Morley. Julius Wangenheim spoke of the foliage remaining green the entire year as a symbol of the perpetual affection for Mr. Morley; that the test of a well spent life is that a city is better for one having lived there. "This," he said, "is the finest example in the world of the building of a park."

Morley Drive and Morley Field in Balboa Park are named to honor this great man.

Building An Exposition

The site chosen for the exposition was 400 acres of high and comparatively level ground, so situated that it would permit almost unlimited expansion beyond its own confines, should the growth of the exposition demand this. The large site was made necessary because Director Collier, who had set about getting state and foreign exhibits at once, found that many more than had been anticipated, wished to exhibit. This was true especially among the countries to the south. Representative Eugenio Dahne came from Brazil and amazed fair officials at the large exhibit he promised, and he felt other South American republics would do as much. Japan gave Collier promise of the largest industrial exhibit it had ever made.

The plan showed the main entrance to the grounds at Laurel and Sixth Avenue, then called Park Avenue. The exposition buildings would

Buildings near completion, 1915

rise beyond the Cabrillo bridge, yet to be built, and would surround a rectangular court. From the gate at Laurel Street to the eastern perimeter of the grounds would be many ornamental plazas and esplanades. The main buildings would be on a central line with the bridge and would include the California Building and those on Art, Agriculture, Horticulture, Liberal Arts, Machinery, U.S. Government, and Mining exhibits. North of this would be a huge Botanical building with the finest lath house ever built — 600 feet long by 100 feet tall. Surrounding it would be exhibits of different nations, outdoor exhibits of reclamation, conservation, and forestry services of the government. Beyond would be the villages and fields of Indian tribes from Arizona and New Mexico. The cliff dwellers, with their ladders leading to their entrances, the tepees of the plains dweller, would all be represented; the Indians would work on their crafts in this village.

Bertram Goodhue, a New York architect, was employed to design the exposition buildings. He later designed the State Capitol Building at Lincoln, Nebraska, the California Institute of Technology, the Naval Training Center and the Marine Base in San Diego. Together with Carleton Winslow, his associate, he created a white walled city of the old Spanish type; some buildings resembled the missions in Southern California; some were like government structures in Mexico or Spain. Everywhere was the Spanish touch, with tiled domes and towers, arched colonnades, mission bells, quiet patios, and fountains flowing gently. Working with Goodhue and Winslow were W. Templeton Johnson, Frank P. Allen and J.H. Davis.

The best authorities and specialists in the country had been procured for the exposition. Before any buildings were made, drawings and photographs of the most famous buildings in Mexico and Spain were studied. Spanish Colonial architecture prevailed, and it was said that the finest examples of this style of any place in America were to be found at the exposition. George Marston, chairman of the buildings and grounds committee appointed John C. Olmsted of the Olmsted Brothers of Brookline, Massachusetts, to plan the buildings and grounds. However when the location of the exposition was determined, the company, preferring the southern part of the park, withdrew from the project. Olmsted is credited with suggesting the colonnades and the Spanish Colonial architecture. Frank P. Allen was made Director of Public Works with Paul Thiene as his assistant.

Landscaping proved to be a very great problem. The trees in Balboa Park today stand straight and firm and tall. Yet to produce this beauty, 100,000 holes were drilled or blasted in the hard pan in order to plant them.

Congress had appropriated $5,000,000 for a celebration of the completion of the Panama Canal, and on May 22, 1911, Colonel D.C. Collier appeared before the Committee on Industrial Arts and Expositions in the House of Representatives, hoping to get part of this fund. He said, in part,

"We have secured the services of the best men that money can buy to place in charge of the Exposition. Bertram G. Goodhue of Cram, Goodhue and Ferguson of New York City, who is considered to be the world's foremost authority on Spanish Colonial architecture, will design the buildings. Frank Allen, responsible for the Exposition buildings at the Seattle and Portland Fairs, will be in charge of buildings and grounds. He receives $20,000 a year, and may take any outside work he can handle. San Diego has a population of 40,000. It has the summer climate of Siberia, Alaska, Newfoundland and Nova Scotia, the latitude of Charleston, South Carolina, the winter climate of the Gulf Coast of the United States. The average January temperature is 57; the average July temperature is 67.

"In one year we have raised $1,000,000 by popular subscription for the purpose of holding the Exposition. We have bonded our city for $1,000,000 for improving the Park for Exposition purposes. We have the pluckiest, nerviest, gamest City in the United States, or the world. We raised $600,000 to lend the U.S. Grant Company to finish the hotel, and $100,000 more to furnish it. We levied $750,000 in bonds for a water and sewage system, and $1,250,000 for roads plus 450 miles in San Diego County. Thus, a city of little less than 40,000 has raised a little less than $5,000,000 for public enterprise.

"The President of the Exposition is the son of an ex-president of the United States. John D. Spreckels, Sugar King, is first Vice-President, A.G. Spalding is second Vice-President. Lyman J. Gage, ex-Secretary of the U.S. Treasury, is one of the Directors. The State of California has pledged $250,000 for a building and $250,000 more for exhibits. We have found the finest talent money can buy to put this Fair together. Our Exposition, which will work out problems, demonstrates resources, and the possibilities and future of the southwest, and of Latin America. A chief attraction will be the reclamation and irrigation of forest and arid lands, the gathering of representatives of Indian Tribes in villages to demonstrate their mode of living."

Colonel Collier met with nothing but disappointment. In disgust he finally said, "To Hell with Congress; San Diego has raised $3,000,000 on her own; we won't fight over the lousy $5,000,000. We'll have our own Fair."

On March 31, 1911 an appropriation of $250,000 for a building at the Panama-California Exposition was signed by Governor Hiram Johnson. $50,000 of this would be paid July 1, 1912 for the plans and foundation. The remainder was released by a bill signed on June 7, 1913. Johnson appointed George Marston, Thomas O'Halloran and Louis Wilde to work with the state; Wilde resigned and Johnson named Russell C. Allen in his place.

Bertram Goodhue, c. 1913

The Philosophy Of The Exposition

Director-General Colonel Collier had given much thought to the character of the exposition's exhibits. As the best person to take charge of these, he turned to Edgar L. Hewett, Director of the American Institute of Archaeology, now the School of American Research of Santa Fe, New Mexico. Hewett would be the architect of the exposition exhibits. In a letter, dated November 11, 1911, asking Hewett to undertake this he wrote,

"The purpose of the Panama-California Exposition is to illustrate the progress and possiblity of the human race, not for the Exposition only, but for a permanent contribution to the world's progress. One phase of the exhibit would be the gathering together of the representative tribes of North and South America in what might be called a Congress of the native tribes of the Western Hemisphere. A permanent building would be used for the purpose."

At the exposition, this permanent building was the California Building, built by the State and called the Science and Education Building.

Near the dawn of the exposition, planning negotiations were started with the Smithsonian Institution, the School of American Archeology and other specific bodies. Their cooperation resulted in a distribution of expense. The first condition was that the archaeological specimens collected should remain the property of the public after the exposition closed.

Expeditions were taken to the deserts of the southwest; among the ancient pueblos and the north coastal Indians of the past, and two expeditions were taken into Central and South America. From Guatemala, the monuments now in the Museum of Man were brought back. In the end, more than 5,000 specimens of ancient pottery, wearing apparel and other articles of ethnological value resulted from these expeditions.

The Smithsonian Institution loaned the exposition a most valuable person, Dr. Ales Hrdlicka, curator of the United States National Museum who prepared the exhibits. The Institute granted whatever time he was needed over the three year preparatory period.

In November 1911, Frank P. Allen, Director of Works, placed the order for the needs of the California Building — now the Museum of Man, designed by Bertram Goodhue, and for a part of the architectural composition for the east end of the bridge across Cabrillo Canyon. The Board of Directors and the Park Commission had adopted the building plans at the November meeting. The Administration building would cost $30,000 and would be ready for occupancy in March, 1912.

The graders were at work on the west park boulevard (Sixth Avenue) at Laurel Street and at the west approach of the bridge where a large amount of filling had to be made. The bridge would be 750 feet in length and 135 feet high. Once work was started, there would be no interruption until it was finished.

An exposition hospital was established on the grounds to take immediate care of injuries and emergencies. Dr. C.L. Caven was the Medical Director. There was a modern surgery department, fully equipped. The hospital equipment was contributed by a large company and shipped, free of charge, to the exposition grounds, to be taken away also free of charge, when it was no longer needed. A mill was built on the grounds to facilitate construction. It was completely fitted with high speed machinery which could do all of the needed work.

In 1912, 50,000 shrubs were planted and lath houses were enlarged to contain more than a million and a half plants for future use. The mill turned out 35,000 plant boxes, from two inches in diameter to four feet square.

Much credit is due the horticulturists of Balboa Park. Fred Bodey worked in preparation for both San Diego expositions. He was largely responsible for planting Palm Canyon.

The San Diego Exposition News of October, 1912 said,

The theme running through the Exposition will be, "Progress of man and his achievement in the completion of the Panama Canal, evidence of what has been done on the American continent for a period of 3,000 years before Christ, the reproduction of monuments and temples in Yucatan and Cliff Dwellers from New Mexico and Arizona as discovered by Coronado in 1540."

It would be the first time at an exposition that the story of physical man would be represented in an illuminating manner. This theme of "How" or "Process" was carried into the Isthmus or fun zone. A motion picture studio was built where movies were made. The villages — Hawaiian, Chinese and Japanese — all showed a realistic picture of native life. The "Panama Canal Extravaganza" showed in accurate style, on a small scale, the manner in which ships passed through this greatest waterway in history.

Life in old Panama, and the work American genius had done to improve it, was shown. San Diego concessions, in addition to being entertaining, were also instructive. Matter of fact products entertained better when shown in the process of manufacture. Scientific displays entertained better when shown in an understandable form. Everyone enjoys something instructive if he can understand it — such were the guiding criteria of all exhibits.

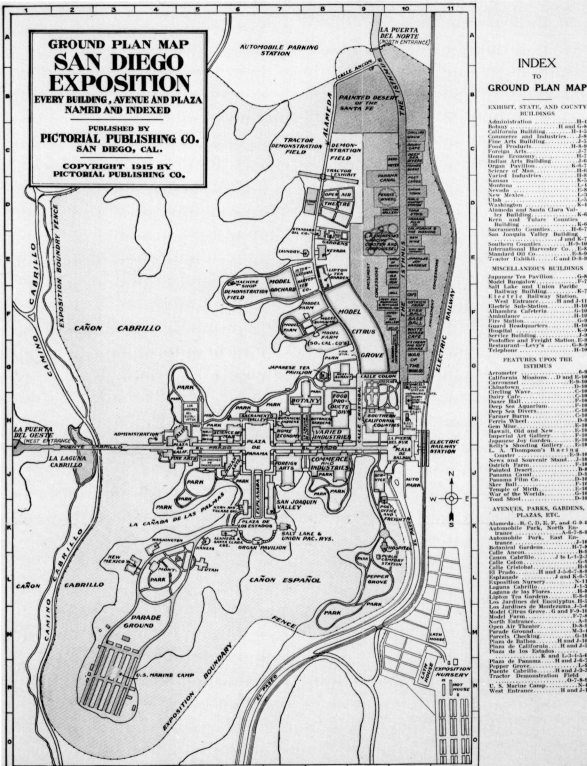

GROUND PLAN MAP
SAN DIEGO EXPOSITION
EVERY BUILDING, AVENUE AND PLAZA NAMED AND INDEXED

PUBLISHED BY
PICTORIAL PUBLISHING CO.
SAN DIEGO, CAL.

COPYRIGHT 1915 BY
PICTORIAL PUBLISHING CO.

INDEX
TO
GROUND PLAN MAP

EXHIBIT, STATE, AND COUNTY BUILDINGS

The ethnology exhibit by the Smithsonian Institution arranged, side by side, models of various epochs showing how slight changes in skull formation brought differing mental and physical conditions.

Model farms for the "Little Landers" were a feature of the horticulture department. A movement was prominent at this time which was called, "Landless Man for the Manless Land." It was planned to have two farms planted during the winter of 1911-12. The ground would be plowed at once. The buildings would be constructed during the winter; each would have a residence, barn and other buildings, small but adequate. The farms would be planted with diversified crops; each would have fruit trees, berries and vegetable gardens. Data would be kept and general average of the whole would be shown. Thus the "Little Landers" would be provided practical information for their contention that a farm of one acre would in twelve years pay for the land, farm buildings and living expenses from farm product income.

Sir Thomas Lipton brought over a tea plantation. The trees were brought from Colombo in glass boxes and 200 young trees were planted to grow and bear during the exposition. Men and women from Colombo came with the trees and took care of them. During the Fair visitors were served tea in a Japanese style tea house. They could witness the entire process: planting the tea trees, stripping and curing the leaves, and, finally, the preparation and brewing of the tea.

The Panama-California Exposition Opens

On the evening of December 31, 1914, Balboa Park was filled with visitors as the Panama-California Exposition prepared to open. Richard U. Dodge in the 1960 *Pacific Railroad Journal* wrote about that night.

"In the final hours of 1914 a large crowd gathered about the organ. J.D. Spreckels was there. Overcome by emotion he said to John F. Forward, President of the Park Commission, simply, 'I beg you to accept this gift on behalf of the people of San Diego.' And thus the unique, the great, the magnificent outdoor pipe organ and its beautiful pavilion were dedicated. Dr. Humphrey J. Stewart had the honor of playing on that memorable night.

"At the stroke of midnight, Pacific Time, Woodrow Wilson, President of the United States, pressed a button in Washington, D.C., which turned on the lights and the Panama California Exposition was formally opened."

Frank Allen had everything in readiness. The exposition was out of debt and in an array of color. Yellow and red were symbols of the exposition, they were seen everywhere. More than 40,000 poinsettia plants were in full bloom. Acacia trees were blooming, and supplied the yellow color. Oxalis was used for borders. Bougainvillea of red and yellow climbed over the buildings. The workers at the fair were in Spanish costumes; in their red and yellow skirts were Spanish dancers; their partners wore short Spanish jackets and white sashes. The guards and attendants were called caballeros and conquistadores. Even the new Cabrillo bridge was flanked on each side with huge urns, out of which rose the century plant, its bloom extending up twenty feet and displaying its yellow blossom. Mariachi bands serenaded, and Ernest Kaii brought from Hawaii, fifty-three natives chosen for their musical talents and for their folk songs. Indians produced their own type of music.

Exhibitors had been carefully screened. "Show them the wheels going round" had been the requirement of bringing products to the fair. In the Commerce and Industries Building were the modern industrial and commercial applications of electricity; a sub-station lighted the grounds and showed how electricity was generated. In the machinery exhibit, every piece turned out a product. The mining exhibit showed mining and the use of the products. The mine was shown operating, and there were shaft tunnels. Several kinds of mining were shown, as was the art of assaying metal, of smelting and other operations.

A small menagerie was located in the area of what is now Park Boulevard, and from this small beginning grew the famous San Diego Zoo. The California Building was the site of the Smithsonian display under Dr. Ales Hrdlicka, which depicted the Mayan culture.

In addition to the educational emphasis of the fair exhibits, each day's program had special events of a cultural nature.

The City of San Diego provided the structure facing the California Building, and these two were the only ones built for lasting use, save the Spreckels Organ Pavilion. The south building was used for an Art Gallery, San Diego's first. Artists and writers were honored, their names given to days at the fair. There were lectures by George Wharton James who spoke of the history of the area. A day was set aside as Estudillo Day in honor of José Estudillo, President of the Town Council at the time the resolution was adopted dedicating Balboa Park. At the time of the exposition he was living in San Jacinto; he came to the fair where the honor accorded made him proud and happy.

California Building, 1915

One of the most beautiful edifices of the fair was the Spreckels Organ Building, built as a great peristyle, as a temple to this masterpiece of musical instrument, the outdoor organ. The building and organ were the gifts of Adolph and John Spreckels to the people of San Diego. Among the artists who sang from the stage, accompanied by the organ, was Madame Ernestine Schumann-Heink. On the occasion of one of her appearances, a printer's error in a newspaper account ended with, "She's golrious." This gave rise to a new word for the duration of the fair.

True western hospitality was extended fair visitors, and they were protected from any form of price-gouging. The directors had a carefully compiled list of hotels, apartments and rooms, with prices listed. To make sure these quoted rates would not be increased, a promise was exacted from each owner that there would be no deviation in rates. New restaurants opening on the exposition grounds had to submit menus and prices, and these had to be approved.

In an article found in the *Sunset* magazine by J. Constantine Hillman called, "On Four Wheels to the Fair," is an account of what one couple found on a visit to the Exposition. Before leaving for the fair, they honestly expected and prepared for greatly inflated prices. Upon arrival they visited the Exposition Bureau and were given two choices of accommodations. They chose one on Laurel Street, two blocks from the park entrance. There was a sweeping view of the ocean and bay. The price per day for the room for the two, including a garage for their car, was $1.00. In late afternoon they went to the fair and paid fifty cents each to enter. The late sun threw a golden glow over the towers and buildings ahead, and the "unforgettable experience cast a spell over the beholder." The effect of the assemblage of the buildings, their relationship to one another, the spacings, the proportioning of the plazas, the soft variations of height all served to satisfy the eye.

The beautiful effect of the gardens at the fair was accomplished by the many workmen, on duty throughout the night transplanting shrubs. At daybreak another crew went to work watering the plants until nine in the morning when the gates opened. Men employed during the day were kept on the hills and canyons where they were scarcely noticed; moreover they were dressed in green sweaters and kaki trousers so that they were scarcely distinguishable from the shrubbery.

The fair was embellished with 2,000,000 plants of 1,200 varieties. There were 350 kinds of trees and shrubs, 85 kinds of vines and 18 varieties of roses. Visitors remarked that it was amazing how the master gardener blended the right flower with the shrubbery of a district; how he displayed

Varied Industries Building, 1915

Buildings along El Prado, 1915 (looking east)

Exposition gardens, 1915

plants and flowers of uniform growth on shady or sunny sides of the building, and how he could, with such skill, transplant immense pepper, eucalyptus or palm trees so that they thrived as if they had been planted for half a century.

One of the greatest charms of the exposition was the hospitality extended. There were no "Keep off the Grass" signs. Visitors found an abundance of benches placed on grassy lawns where they might rest. The Women's Headquarters was planned and furnished by the Women's Official Exposition Board. A large reception room, one of the finest in the exposition, was done in persimmon red, black and gray which gave the warmth of color typical of Spain and the southwest, and emanated hospitality.

The decorations were the work of Alice Klauber who added a further touch by having real persimmons hanging from their branches in jardinieres. Rocking chairs were dressed with velvet cushions; there were red draperies, oriental hangings and a desk made of an old piano, painted red. An eastern woman, charmed by this wired home, told her family not to sell the old piano, that she would make a desk out of it. There was a quiet room on the first floor of the Women's Headquarters with cots for resting, and beds for emergencies. A trained nurse was in charge. Someone said, "The men put up the buildings, the women followed and decorated them." Bright colored curtains and drapes throughout the buildings did much to enhance

Alice Klauber

Indian Arts Building, 1915

*Indian Arts
Building with
its Mission
Bell arch*

the white architecture of the fair. There were pretty spots for entertaining the visiting women.

In the Fine Arts Building, the Daughters of the American Revolution had a room where they used blue and white coverlets as portiers; these were all hand woven. They used rag rugs and an odd little piano — one of the first upright pianos ever built. They had a spinning wheel and a grandfather clock — all of which made the room attractive. The members served as hostesses to women visitors. Another comfort room was provided for mothers with babies.

The Women's Christian Temperance Union furnished a rest and recreation room for girls who were employed at the fair. They had information on hotels and lodging houses for women who traveled alone. A representative worked with young women, and looked after them while they visited the fair.

Many noted persons visited the exposition, among them William Howard Taft, Theodore Roosevelt, William Jennings Bryan and Thomas Edison. Former President Theodore Roosevelt said:

"It is so beautiful that I wish to make an earnest plea that you keep these buildings of rare phenomenal taste and beauty permanently. I hope that you of San Diego will recognize what so many other communities have failed to recognize: That beauty is not only worth while for its own sake, but it is valuable commercially,"

Secretary of Navy, Josephus Daniels and his assistant, Franklin D. Roosevelt were in the first car to travel over the Cabrillo Bridge. In Aubrey Davidson's account of the fair he told of taking Secretary of the Navy Daniels on a tour of San Diego Bay. Daniels said, "You have enough water here to float every naval vessel in the world. What are you doing with it?" To which Davidson replied that if the government would dredge the bay and send the Navy to San Diego, the city would render all possible aid.

Lily Pond looking towards El Prado

COLLECTED BY DR. EUGENIO DAHNE

THE HEALTHIES

PURE COFFEE

G COUNTRY IN THE WORLD
OR 1,500 MILLION POUNDS

IN THE WORLD

FFEE

NG COFFEE AT SANTOS

BRA

BRAZIL

Coffee

Mate

William Jennings Bryan (next to woman in white) at the Brazilian products exhibit

The Dibold family at the exposition, July 18, 1916

Miss San Diego (opposite, top) at the 1916 exposition

The Liberty Bell came from Philadelphia to the Fair for three days. In all, more than 3,000,000 visitors attended the exposition.

Many benefits came to San Diego, due in large part to the Panama-California Exposition. The Naval Training Center moved from Goat Island in San Francisco Bay to its present site in San Diego. North Island was purchased by the government and became a great air center. The Marine Base was constructed and the Destroyer Base was established. The Naval Hospital was built in Balboa Park. "San Diego reaped more benefit than any of us dreamed of."

G. Aubrey Davidson said that the great success of the fair came from the loyalty of every member of the Exposition Board and from the San Diego citizenry. He spoke of U.S. Grant, Jr., the first president; of Colonel D. C. Collier, director-general, and the creative genius of the exposition, John D. Spreckels, a tower of strength; George W. Marston, chairman of Buildings and Grounds, R.C. Allen of the same committee; George Burnham who received distinguished guests, Frank J. Belcher and Julius Wangenheim who managed the finances, and Carl H. Heilbron who did public speaking and managed special days and social events.

William Kettner, who served on the harbor commission and as a representative in Congress was credited with obtaining much of the federal help for the city and exposition.

The Fair Is Re-Organized For 1916

At the end of a successful year, Spreckels, Burnham, Heilbron and Davidson were the only members of the Board who wished to prolong the fair for another year. They were the nucleus who organized the 1916 exposition. After an appeal was made to Los Angeles for financial assistance, a subscription of $250,000 was pledged by commercial and industrial leaders of that city.

In 1916 it was named the *Panama-California International Exposition* although *International* was not used in every reference to the second year of the exposition.

For the year of 1916 the officers were:

President, G.A. Davidson; First Vice-President, Robert N. Bulla of Los Angeles; Second Vice-President, John D. Spreckels; Third Vice-President, Edwin M. Capps; Fourth Vice-President, Carl H. Heilbron; Fifth Vice-President, John F. Forward, Jr.; Secretary, H.H. Penfold and Treasurer, Frank C. Spalding.

The Directors for the 1916 Fair were:

E.M. Capps, Mayor; C.T. Chandler, J. Fred Schlingman, H.J. Penfold, John D. Spreckels, L.J. Wilde, S.R. Flynn, John Forward, Jr., G.A. Davidson, Colonel Ed Fletcher, Harry L. Titus, J.P. Smith, L.R. Barrows, Lane D. Webber, Carl F. Ferris, James MacMullen, Colonel Fred Jewell, Carl H. Heilbron, Duncan MacKinnon, Colonel D.C. Collier and Judge W.A. Sloane.

Directors from Los Angeles were: Robert N. Bulla, Vernon Goodwin, S.L. Weaver, John S. Mitchell, Fred L. Baker, J.O. Koepfli, M.A. Hamburger, C.D. Hamilton, R.W. Pridman and E.J. Eisenmeyer.

For the second year, since San Francisco's fair was ended, the Canadian exhibit was obtained, as well as those from France, Germany, Holland, Spain, Brazil and other nations. Nine states erected state buildings, some of which still stand.

The Fourth Marine Regiment, commanded by

Colonel Joseph H. Pendleton, established a camp on North Island in 1914. He later became a Major General, and Camp Pendleton was named in his honor. The island camp was abandoned in 1914 when the regiment was assigned to duty at the Panama-California Exposition in Balboa Park and to the Panama-Pacific Exposition in San Francisco.

The United States gave a special recognition to the 1916 exposition. A troop of cavalry, a battalion of infantry, the Coast Guard artillery and many bands were ordered to San Diego. The Pacific Fleet kept in sight of the grounds. In addition, nineteen more counties had exhibits installed during January and February. The formal dedication occurred on May 18th. It was said that no Midway ever compared to that of the 1915-1916 exposition.

At the end, the exposition was able to pay all expenses. There was money left, and this was given to the San Diego Museum. The accomplishments of the fair were far-reaching. The city's growth was greatly affected: many new residents came to the city from their experiences at the exposition, or from stories told about it. In exhibits the exposition had shown a vast amount of the practical, combined with the romantic and historical. Thus, was demonstrated the spirit of Southern California, portraying ever the combination of the practical with the poetic.

San Francisco and San Diego had forgotten their animosity, and worked closely together during the 1915 fair. This resulted in a warm and lasting regard between these two cities. The railroads had given great assistance by making round trip fares to the west to include both cities at no extra cost, thus enabling and encouraging tourists to visit both expositions. On the night of January 1, 1917, Madame Ernestine Schumann-Heink sang "Auld Lang Syne" from the stage of the beautiful organ. Fireworks spelled out "World Peace 1917." The Band played "The Star Spangled Banner," and the Panama-California Exposition was declared closed.

In just three months, the United States would declare war on Germany.

Overview of Balboa Park and the 1915 Panama-California Exposition

Courtesy, Daryl Collins

Children's Day at the 1916 exposition with Huber A. Collins as the Pied Piper of Hamlin

Courtesy, Estelle Finster

Buildings And Features Remaining From The 1915-16 Exposition

For illustrations of these buildings and for descriptions of those which were built to last at the most two years—and since have been demolished—two excellent books are recommended: *The Architecture and Gardens of the San Diego Exposition,* by Bertram Goodhue, and *The San Diego Garden Fair* by Eugen Neuhaus. These books are available in the California Room at the San Diego Public Library.

The 1915 exposition buildings portrayed a story of monumental archaeology in southwestern America from the discovery to the end of the Spanish rule. In the history of the park, little mention is made of those buildings which at this time are no longer in existence. The people of San Diego have shown great reluctance to part with them. The beautiful California Building, and the lower building to the south, remain as an imposing nucleus for whatever further developments may accrue to the park.

The **Cabrillo Bridge,** an extraordinary structure spanning the Cabrillo Canyon, was the first multiple arched, cantilever type bridge built in California. By cantilever, it is meant that the tops of the bridge, over each arch, lock into place from the piers and toward each other. Each of the seven piers sustains the weight of one half arch on either side. One inch of space is left between each unit for expansion. Each pier then becomes a unit. The structural engineer for the bridge was Thomas B. Hunter, who was with the California Division of Public Works. It was built by Frank P. Allen at a cost of $214,000 and is 1505 feet long, including the approaches. The length of the bridge itself is 405 feet, and the height has been given as 125 feet.

> "Of the many structures built in preparation for the great fair, one of the most functional was Cabrillo Bridge. With a great ceremony the bridge was dedicated April 12, 1914 and the first person to ride across it was Franklin D. Roosevelt then Assistant Secretary of the Navy, 22 years later he would be the one president elected 4 terms in succession."

In June of 1950 a fence was erected on either side of the bridge, made necessary because up to that time fifty persons had jumped to their death from the bridge. On one morning after several of these suicides, some wag posted a sign beside the roadway beneath the bridge reading, "Beware of falling bodies." In the 1930s a sailor leaped from the bridge, landed on his head in

Called "the most beautiful woman in California" Mrs. Maude Estelle Compton was married at the exposition on August 18, 1916

Cabrillo Bridge and pond, 1915

the lily pond, got up, wiped the mud from his face, and went away talking to himself. In 1951 a fire was started in the bridge. Up to that time, it had been possible to enter the west end of the bridge, and rubbish collected there. It was thought a cigarette was responsible for the fire. The entrance has since been sealed.

Vines cover some of the piers, and the trees on the slope of the canyon's east and west banks blend in gracefully for views of the bridge taken from north or south. Standing on the south walk of Cabrillo Bridge affords a splendid view of the city skyline, the bay, ocean, bridge with Coronado beyond.

The **Administration Building,** of Spanish Colonial style, is lower in design than the ones to the east, and this has the effect of softening

the abruptness which otherwise would be apparent in approaching the Museum of Man. It is situated directly at the end of Cabrillo Bridge on the north side of El Prado, as Laurel Street is called within the Park.

Built at a cost of $30,000, it was probably designed by Irving Gill, although Carleton Monroe Winslow was also responsible for a portion of the design. Frank P. Allen had charge of construction. It was the first of the exposition buildings to be completed and was the headquarters for the Panama-California Exposition. Afterward it was used by Park Department personnel, as a city water-testing laboratory, by the San Diego Bureau of Mines and by the Division of Recreation Projects under the Works Progress Administration. The building later served as headquarters for the 1935-36 exposition when it was also used as a police sub-station. With the rest of the park buildings, it was turned over to the navy during the Second World War.

Entering the Park from the west, the approach to The **West Gate** from the bridge reminds one of entering many European cities. The effect has been likened to that of a rich and dignified entrance to a Spanish City. The deep archway is characterized by columns on either side, described as Doric orders; to the architect this is a part of a well known nomenclature; to the usual reader, a Doric order is a plain column, and the part above, called the capital, is also plain. The entablature—or the upper part of the gateway resting on the column—is decorated with carvings enclosed in spandrels, (the enclosure formed by the upper and lower angles).

The enclosed space created by the north and south wings of the Museum of Man and the west and east gates is called the Plaza de California. On the wall facing the steps to the north, the bas-relief of D.C. Collier has been described. Across the driveway is another bas-relief of the *San Salvador,* Cabrillo's ship. "To commemorate the Discovery of California by Juan Rodriguez Cabrillo, who landed on the shores of San Diego Bay, September 28, 1542." Placed by the San Diego Chapter, Daughters of the American Revolution. 1921.

The **Inside Gateway** (or east gateway) of the California Quadrangle is in reality a part of the California Building, now the Museum of Man. In the center over the doorway, is the Coat of Arms of California. On the left side of the California Seal are the words *AEDIFICATO ANNO,* and on the right side, *SALUTIS MD CCCCXV,* Latin words and Roman numerals denoting the year in which the building was finished. The spandrels (enclosures) to the right and left of the doorway on the south side are filled with colored tile commemorating the beginning of Spanish occupation with the motto of Spain and the date of 1769. To the right or north side are the Seal of the United States and the date 1846, the year this area became a part of the United States, and the date of the Constitutional Convention in Monterey.

The **California Building** is considered to be outstanding among all the park buildings. Some have said that it is one of the finest examples of Renaissance Spanish architecture in existence.

The design was the work of Bertram Goodhue and his associate, Carleton S. Winslow. The State of California supplied $500,000 for the building and exhibits. The two structures enclosing all sides of the square, form what is called the California Quadrangle. The California Building has two sure characteristics of

Spanish or Mexican design:
1. A tower or *Campanile* and
2. An ornamental frontspiece.

The tower of the building is 200 feet tall; the lower part is rather plain and pierced by a few small windows. The upper part consists of three belfry stories surmounted by a bell-shaped dome which is encircled by a cincture (girdle of containment), and completed with a great iron weathervane in the shape of a Spanish ship, much like the one used by Cabrillo. The design of the building is similar to the Tepotzotlan Cathedral a few miles out of Mexico City.

A great dome topped with a Spanish cross is tiled in geometric design, as are the smaller domes. This tile was designed by Walter Nordhoff in National City after extensive study of Spanish Moorish ceramics. About the base of the great dome is an inscription taken from Dueteronomy 8:8 which reads:

"A land of wheat and barley and vines and fig trees, a land of olive trees and honey."

A window in the east wall is especially noteworthy. Divided into casement type portions, the

The West Gate was designed to represent the Atlantic and Pacific Oceans joined by the completion of the Panama Canal

The top of the gate displays the Crest of San Diego; the figure on the left: Atlantic; the figure on the right: Pacific

Tower of the California Building

Figures on the face of the California Building—

At the very top is a statue of Father Junípero Serra. Above his head is the shield of the United States

Left (West Side) top to bottom:

1. *Bust of Philip III of Spain*

2. *Coat of Arms of Spain*

3. *Sebastián Vizcaíno who rediscovered San Diego Bay in 1602*

4. *George Vancouver, who sailed into San Diego Bay in 1783*

5. *Father Luis Jayme, California's first Christian martyr, who was killed at Mission San Diego*

Right (East Side) top to bottom:

1. *Bust of Carlos III of Spain*

2. *Coat of Arms of Mexico*

3. *Statue of Juan Rodríguez Cabrillo, who discovered San Diego Bay in 1542*

4. *Bust of Gaspar de Portolá, first Spanish governor of California*

5. *Father Antonio de la Ascención a cartographer for Sebastián Vizcaíno*

panes are mullioned—divided into small panes by leaded bars. The window is surrounded by an ornate frame, above which is the Seal of California; below is the word "Eureka," the California state motto which is interpreted to mean, "I have found it."

The architecture of the building is Spanish Colonial, as was the motif of all the 1915 exposition buildings. The quadrangle formed by the two buildings is characteristic of such structures in Italy or Mexico.

Across to the south from the Museum of Man is the low mission-style building which was provided by the City of San Diego at a cost of $75,000. Although a sharp contrast in height and simplicity, the two buildings harmonize perfectly. In this low building the windows are port holes, and it is roofed with vigas (wooden logs) in early Mission style. During the Panama-California Exposition, a collection of paintings,

lent by the French Government, was housed in this building and it was known as the Fine Arts Building. It was San Diego's first art gallery.

The beautifully designed face of the building is devoted to characters and emblems which have all been a part of the early history of San Diego. At the very top stands the figure of Fr. Junípero Serra, a Franciscan padre, who founded on July 16, 1769, the Mission San Diego de Alcalá. This date became the birthday of the city of San Diego. Above the head of Fr. Serra is the shield of the United States.

The MUSEUM OF MAN, now housed within the California Building, is "devoted to research, interpretation and exhibition of material which will illuminate the understanding of human origins."

At the close of the Panama-California Exposition the California Building was given over to the "San Diego Museum" to continue the work started by the acquisition of the original exhibits. The San Diego Museum was incorporated by the State of California on November 3, 1915. In 1926 the State of California which had, up to this time, owned and maintained the building released it to the city government. The San Diego Museum became the Museum of Man in 1942.

In rooms beneath the museum are thousands of articles collected for preservation, study and research. This department produces publications of two kinds: Ethnic Technology Notes and the San Diego Museum Papers.

The **Chapel of St. Francis,** located in the southwest corner of the Plaza de California (the square space formed by the Museum of Man), presents "the typical characteristics of a true Mission interior." According to Eugen Neuhaus from whose *The San Diego Garden Fair* this description is taken, the chapel was named for, and dedicated to, Fr. Junípero Serra. All other authorities call it, "St. Francis Chapel."

A truly religious atmosphere pervades this little chapel; of stark simplicity, the center of interest is the beautiful frontispiece while the other few furnishings are simple. Like the great frontispiece of the Museum of Man, the Great Altar presents sculptured figures of religious historical interest. The most prominent statue in the center is that of Our Lady and Child. At the left stands the somber figure of St. Francis Xavier, patron of the Jesuits and introduced to commemorate the Missions in Arizona and their founders. At the right is the statue of an unknown secular priest or saint commemorating the work of the church in California. The two heads above are of Santa Isabel (St. Elizabeth) of Hungary, identified by the crown; and on the other side, Santa Clara of Assisi, founder of the second Order of Franciscans,

and friend of San Francisco. The heads of the two bishops below are those of San Buenaventura, Bishop of Albano, and San Luis, Bishop of Tolosa (St. Louis of Tolouse), both Franciscans and patrons of California missions.

The Chapel of St. Francis has never been dedicated. It was used extensively for a chapel by the Navy during the Second World War. It is used today often for weddings, with no designation of sectarianism.

The **House of Charm** displays the almost primitive simplicity of the Spanish Colonial Mission style. The east side of the fachada (or elevation) consists of a central arch flanked by two bell towers of gables of uneven height and design, one mounting three bells, the other two. At the northeast corner, the Carmelite belfry is an accentuated arch of the arcade, or portales facing the prado. These portales or arcades used in the architecture, give more Spanish character to the buildings than do any other single detail. The building was designed by Carleton Winslow and H.L. Schmohl supervised construction. It is said to resemble the Basilica de Guadalupe in Guadaljara, Mexico.

The south side of the Plaza de Panama is partly enclosed by arcades abutting what is now the House of Charm and the House of Hospitality. Built for the 1915 exposition, the House of Charm was called the Indian Arts Building. During the second year when the exposition in San Francisco had closed, exhibits from that fair were brought directly to this building. In 1925 the building was bare, save for a single refreshment stand.

During the 1935-36 exposition, it was named the House of Charm, and various souvenirs and small gift type of articles were for sale there. Aside from repairs after the Second World War, this building has never undergone any large program of renovation. When it was reopened in 1948, many large flower shows were held there.

An organization that is currently housed in the House of Charm is the SAN DIEGO ART INSTITUTE. The purpose of the San Diego Art Institute is: "to encourage the growth and development of Fine Arts within the community; to foster the expression of artistic talent within the membership; and to engage in such educational activities as will advance the objectives." The corporation is non-political, non-sectarian, non-profit. Organized by Dr. Reginald Poland, Director of the Fine Arts Gallery; founded in 1941 as the San Diego Business Men's Art Club; the chief objective, originally, was to paint characteristic and historic scenes of San Diego and vicinity. Walter W. Austin, former mayor of San Diego served as first president. In 1951 the group reorganized to become the San Diego Men's Art Institute.

Women were accepted as members. Two years later the present location in the House of Charm was chosen; the group re-incorporated as the San Diego Art Institute.

The **Balboa Park Club** was built by the State of New Mexico for the 1915 exposition. The famous Church of Acoma was used as a suggestion for the design. This Mission Church was built by the Franciscan padres and the local Indians and Spanish settlers in 1529. The State of New Mexico employed the Rapp Brothers of Trinidad, Colorado to design and construct the building. The two tower effect is seen in the original church; the pueblo style of architecture was emphasized in the irregular walls and rough beams. The style of the now Balboa Park Club may be seen in Santa Fe New Mexico today. Exposition visitors from that state were so enthusiastic about their New Mexico building that, a few years later, when the New Mexico Museum of Fine Arts was erected a similar design was used. In 1922-23 the building was scheduled to be torn down but a group of artists asked to use it. An Art Center under direction of Kanuela Searle was established and in 1923 the Art School and building were placed under the control of the San Diego Museum.

In preparation for the second exposition, the building received extensive enlargement and remodelling. During 1935-36 it was the Palace of Education. A large mural covers the west wall of the entrance hall. The artist's name—Belle Baranceanu—is to be found in the lower right hand corner. The mural depicts a figure of youth in the upper center; symbols of time to the right are the sphinx, the hour glass, the clock and the calendar. Man's earliest form of expression—cave painting—and the progress of learning through agriculture, trains, boats, factories, the printing press, astronomy, science, aviation, are also represented. In addition, progress in education is shown in machinery, law and the arts; war, industry, architecture, communication, schools and university. All of these facets of youth and education are to be seen in this mural of the 1930s.

The Schweigardt Fountain in the center of the room is named the "Four Corners of American Democracy." Each of the four corners is represented by one of more figures:

Community: a figure with outstretched hands.

Church: A figure in the attitude of prayer.

Home: Shown by a figure of mother and child.

School: A child with a book.

And high over the fountain is the figure of a dancing child, which is universally accepted as a symbol of crowning happiness.

Courtyard of the House of Hospitality after 1935 remodeling

Following the close of the second exposition, the building was leased by a group known as the "Hall of Education Association." Rooms and halls were rented to various groups. Classes in art, china painting, and vocal music were conducted in the building. Claremont Colleges of Pomona conducted a Seminar here. It was used extensively as an exhibit hall. The music program of the W.P.A. was centered here, and orchestras used the space for practice. During the Second World War it was known as the Admiral Kidd Officers Club, named for Admiral Isaac C. Kidd who died at Pearl Harbor. It was the last building to be returned to the city from the Navy after World War II. Restoration of the building cost $75,000, which included new furnishings for the lounge. The dance floor capacity in the building is 2250, and 1250 may be seated at one time for dinners. The kitchen is large and well equipped. On April 22, 1948 the building was named Balboa Park Club. With other structures in this area it was renovated and greatly improved in 1972.

The **House of Hospitality** on the southeast corner of Plaza de Panama is a community center where San Diegans and their visitors may meet for social, educational, and cultural purposes, such as lectures, musicals, receptions, dancing, luncheons, teas, dinners and banquets.

The building, with its adequate facilities for conducting these various gatherings, is under

the supervision of a group of civic minded men and women operating under the name of House of Hospitality Association. During the 1915 exposition this was the Foreign Arts Building. During the 1935-36 exposition, it served as headquarters for the Women's Executive Committee, an organization formed to create a fine cultural, social and civic center in the heart of the beautiful Park. This ornate structure was designed by Carleton Winslow, and is said to resemble the Hospital of Santa Cruz in Toledo, Spain. The corner tower, by being set at the back line of the portales, gains interest and importance.

The heraldic decorations (historical symbols) found over the archways and entrances represent the Coats of Arms of the various countries in the Pan American Union which participated in the Exposition, and at the top and center of the main pavilion is the Seal of the Pan American Union. As with all of the exposition buildings, embodiments of more than one famous building in Spain or Mexico may be found in similarity to the House of Hospitality. For example, the fountains and garden are designed from a Spanish Palace called the Casa del Rey Moro (House of the Moorish King). Before the 1935 exposition, the Park Board took the fire insurance money collected after the Civic Auditorium burned, and used this to renovate the former Foreign Arts Building.

The firm of Requa, Jackson and Hamill undertook the very extensive remodelling and Sam Hamill has been given full credit for the beauty which resulted from this great project. The building of the 1915 fair was T shaped and had an extension to the south where now is the outside dining area and the garden. This was removed. The lovely patio within was created by cutting an area from the center of the building. This created a structure, new, functional, and unique in design. Across the ceiling of the second story as seen through the graceful arches extend the heavy timbers, remainders of those which originally spanned the building.

The architecture and landscaping of the garden show both the Spanish and Moorish influences. The patio of the House of Hospitality is surrounded by typically Spanish arcades. Colored lanterns project from the walls of the court; near one corner is a wishing well, a replica of one in the Guadalajara Museum Gardens. In the center is a tiled fountain dominated by a seated figure of La Tehuana of Tehuantepec, Mexico by Donal Hord. This was made from Indiana limestone; more than half of a 1200 pound block of the rock was chiseled away during the ten weeks of persistent and documentary work to produce the rounded feminine figure. Donal Hord began carving as a

teenage boy ill with rheumatic fever. Later when his health improved he studied at the School of Arts in Santa Barbara. His ability was outstanding. He received an exchange scholarship for further study and spent more than a year travelling and working in Mexico. In 1929 he attended the American Academy of the Arts in Philadelphia and followed this study with a period at the Beaux Arts in New York. Here he turned his attention to the architectural use of sculpture. His work is seen in many places in San Diego. Homer Dana became associated with Donal Hord in the 1920s and provided the physical strength needed to carry out the designs of the master sculptor. This use of a Hord sculpture of the native Mexican woman, in the House of Hospitality patio, as beautifully designed by San Diego architect Sam Hamill seems altogether fitting; they belong together.

On the north side of the patio are a number of rooms, some with kitchen facilities to accommodate various size meetings. The main auditorium which faces the patio on the east has a maple floor, excellent acoustics and unusual lighting accessories. The ornate entrance to the auditorium was done by Rose Hanks. It is used for dances, large parties, plays, lectures and musicales. The adjoining lounge serves small parties, recitals and is used with the auditorium. A popular room, especially adapted for teas and musicales, is the Loggia on the second floor. It seats 150 persons and is bright and airy with open balconies on both sides affording views of the Park. The Cafe del Rey Moro is a park restaurant and a delightful location for dining. One of the most popular attractions is the open air terrace on the south where, in good weather and under bright canopies, meals are served throughout the year.

The Sala de Oro is a Spanish type reception room, a favorite meeting place for diners or social functions. The carved sacristy cabinet of early Italian workmanship on the west wall is especially interesting.

During the Second World War, the House of Hospitality was converted into a nursing center, and as many as 600 nurses were housed in the building. In 1947, when the City recovered it, $80,000 was spent for restoration, and $40,000 for furnishings. It was reopened in December 1948. In 1967, the Junior League enlisted the aid of the city, the Architects Association and other groups and, spending a large amount from their own resources redecorated the building.

The **Botanical Building and Lily Pond** were built for the first exposition in 1915. The Lily Pond (or Laguna, as it was named) stretches south of the Botanical Building and at the north end is a balustraded bridge separating the pond in two. The bridge has great ornamental flower containers on either end. The lotus water lily is the flower most used in the pond.

The Botanical Building was designed by Carleton Winslow and Frank P. Allen supervised the construction. It was closed for some time during and after the First World War. During the Second War when the Navy took over most of the park, the lily pond became a swimming pool for patients of the Navy Hospital. During the summer of 1945, the lily pond swimming pool was open to the city children, and 22,286 youngsters used it. The Botanical Building stood closed and neglected until it was reopened on July 1, 1957 after an extensive renovation and remodeling.

Seventy thousand lineal feet of redwood lath, or more than twelve miles, were used in the remodeling, at a cost of $63,500. Below an eight foot height, the redwood is 2½ inches wide and 1½ inches thick, for added strength. Above eight feet, the boards are ½ inch thick. At the time of the reopening, there were no funds available for plants, and local nurseries came forward with large donations of exhibits for the building.

At present the city-owned nursery supplies most of the exhibits. These are changed often to seasonal displays of expertly arranged plants and flowers. The building houses many rare and beautiful plants.

On February 25, 1964, Robert M. Golden, prominent San Diego construction executive, announced that he would renovate the fifty year old balustrade which divides the lily pond plus the massive flower containers which stood on the ends of the balustrade. This face-lifting made a remarkable improvement in the approach.

The Botanical Building has become famous for seasonal displays of flowers. Tulips are featured in the spring, lilies at Easter, at Christmas, the beautiful poinsettias are shown.

The Botanical Building and Lily Pond as they were in 1915

The Spreckels Organ and Organ Pavilion, 1915

On May 27, 1968, a group of officers and men from the *U.S.S. Constellation* held a presentation and dedication ceremony before this balustrade as they presented to the city a Memorial Sun Dial which was installed in the north lily pond.

Flanking the lily pond, on either side, are matching fountains installed for the 1915 exposition. These had been unused for many years.

In 1965 the Thursday Club restored the fountain on the west side and in 1967 a group of ten women restored the east fountain.

The **Spreckels Organ** and **Organ Pavilion** were presented to the people of San Diego for the 1915 exposition by John D. and Adolph B. Spreckels. The cost of the structure was $100,000, the organ $33,500. The organ is housed in an ornate vaulted structure which is characterized by a proscenium with decorative framework providing beautiful patterns of light and shade, and also with flattened, highly embellished gables. From the central building on either side branch curved colonnaded walks, with approaching steps at each end. These pillars create a Corinthian peristyle effect which partially encloses this open air theater. Benches seat 2000 and, at many functions, temporary raised seats provide for many more. The pavilion was designed by Harrison Albright who also designed the Spreckels Theater. The organ was built by the Austin Organ Company of Hartford, Connecticut.
of Hartford, Connecticut.

John D. Spreckels loved music; he installed a large organ in his home. When he ordered the Austin organ of Balboa Park it was for an entirely different location. He planned to place it in Mission Cliff Gardens, a beautiful little area at the end of his street car line. Exposition directors persuaded him to bring the organ to the Park instead. Spreckels insisted on a north exposure and chose the new location; one which exposition plans had designated for another structure. In return, Spreckels was given a franchise by the city which extended the street car line to the east entrance of the exposition grounds. Spreckels made sizeable donations to the exposition funds both before and after the change in his organ location.

The great organ features an all electric movable console of 4 manuals and it has a vast array of total possibilities and mechanical contrivances. Back of the gold front pipes, visible when the curtain is raised, pipes in 53 sets are arranged in an array in baffled chambers and nearly 3500 of these project the organ sound to great distances.

San Diego is one of the few places in the world where such an organ could function effectively; the city has the smallest mean temperature (difference between the highest and lowest, summer and winter) of anywhere in the world and this is a very great advantage and an important factor toward keeping the organ in tune.

From time to time changes and additions have been made to the organ. In 1935, for the California Pacific International Exposition, a new console and a five rank Great Mixture were added. At this time the stage was doubled in size. Recently, the Committee of 100 gave the organ another new console, new components and raised money to restore the pavilion.

To protect the organ, when it is not in use, is a tremendous metal curtain. When the building was first under construction in 1914, two concrete pillars were built some 40 feet above the rest of the stage level. The metal curtain was then placed on these pillars and the rest of the structure was built about it. The weight of the curtain is believed to be about twelve tons. For years, the curtain was raised and lowered by hand, however in the 1930s the city replaced man-power with an electric motor. Several years ago, a new automatic system was installed. When the weather does not permit an open air performance, it is possible to improvise a small audience hall back stage. In the early years of organ concerts, and before the era of microphones the program was announced by means of a megaphone.

Dr. Humphrey John Stewart (1854-1932) was the first official city organist. He was an Englishman of the old school, was once mayor of Coronado, was a composer of choral, organ and orchestral music and was much loved in the community for his wit and humor.

For many years Royal Albert Brown (1890-1954) was the assistant to Dr. Stewart. When the latter retired in August, 1932, Royal Brown became the official Civic Organist. The slight change in title came about because Dr. Stewart had been paid by the Spreckels Company, while Mr. Brown's pay was assumed by the city. Brown was a graduate of the University of Texas, had studied in Paris, and was an outstanding teacher of organ and piano. He was a devoted musician and riding the La Jolla bus to San Diego, he would arouse sly smiles as he was observed practicing finger exercises, and using his trousers as a key board. Royal Brown was also a composer. A contemporary composer told of the thrill of hearing Mr. Brown play one of her compositions and of seeing her name on the program beside that of Johann Strauss.

After the death of Royal Brown in 1954, Charles Rollin Shatto became the third organist. He served through Labor Day of 1957. Douglas Ian Duncan was appointed organist that fall. He studied at the University of Redlands and later earned a degree in Music and Art from California Western University. For over twenty years Douglas Duncan enhanced the park with his beautiful music but his devotion to the organ and the building go beyond that. Someone passing by caught sight of two men high on ladders replacing electric bulbs in the arch above the stage and discovered Duncan and his technician making these needed repairs.

The first organ technician was Roy W. Tolchard. He was followed by Leonard Dowling, who drove from Santa Monica to oversee every organ performance. The present technician is L.W. Blackinton.

Organist Douglas Duncan was followed by Jared C. Jacobsen. The present organist is Robert Plimpton.

A fountain installed for the 1935-36 exposition, not now used, on the north wall completing the enclosure of the organ pavilion is designed like one on Paseo de Reforma in Mexico City. Above it a brass plaque covers an aperture containing the names of all who worked to prepare the second exposition. The plaque states:

"Herein are the signatures of the workers whose untiring and loyal effort made possible the California-Pacific International Exposition, 1936

On the opposite side of the wall, a brass plaque honors the memory of Mme Schumann-Heink:

Mme Ernestine Schumann-Heink
A Gold Star Mother
A Star of the World.

John D. Spreckels died June 7, 1926. Memorial services for him were held at the Organ Pavilion, music to his memory came from the magnificent organ he gave to the people of San Diego in 1915. On the east side of the audience space of the enclosure stands his bust, mounted on a marble pedestal. The bust was a gift to the park from the widow of the sculptor, James Tank Porter. The Woman's Committee of the San Diego Historical Society provided the plaque to this statue of John D. Spreckels.

The **Hall of Nations** was first the Utah Building during the 1915 exposition; during the next fair it was the press club, during the Second World War it was officers quarters and for many years (1923-1971) it was the home of the San Diego Floral Association. Much of the floral exhibit for the California Pacific International Exposition was planned here.

The **Casa de Balboa**, or **Electric Building** as it has been called, is of modified plateresque style and is thought to resemble the Palace of Government of Querétaro, Mexico, which was built during the 1700s or early in the 1800s. The roof of the building extends nine feet beyond the wall of the building, and it is supported by carved caryatids, or supports, in the form of women.

Pillars with highly decorated cornices form an arcade which connects the building to the west with the House of Hospitality. Above each entrance are three heavily ornamented arch-topped windows. Each has a curved balcony protected by an iron railing. A tower, the top of which is elaborately decorated, stands at the northwest corner of the building.

In the exposition of 1915 this was the Commerce and Industries Building, in the 1916 fair it became the Canadian Building. That year industries, transportation and wild life of Canada were shown. Among the exhibits was a colony of beavers building a dam in a real stream. During the First World War, this was one of the buildings used by the military authorities.

In 1922 on December 9, the San Diego Society of Natural History opened a museum here. During the second exposition the building became the Palace of Better Housing, featuring displays of building materials and model structures. Afterwards, Electric Shows were held frequently, and the name "Electric Building" was adopted in 1936. The Red Cross Headquarters were located in the west wing of the building. In 1942, the Navy took it over as a part of the hospital complex of the Second World War.

After the war $60,000 of Navy funds were spent for restoration and repair, and the city spent $10,000 more for electric modernization and other equipment and the building was reopened.

Between 1949 and 1965, the building housed activities such as home shows, animal shows (dogs and cats), rummage sales, a rehearsal hall, and a folk dance area, to name but a few of them. In June, 1965 the Aero-Space Museum moved into the Electric Building from the Food and Beverage Building. The Hall of Science and the International Aerospace Hall of Fame occupied parts of the Electric Building.

The present structure is a larger duplicate of

The Commerce and Industries Building, 1916 (now renamed The Casa de Balboa)

the original building which was destroyed by arson in 1978. It now houses five tenants: The MUSEUM OF SAN DIEGO HISTORY (operated by the San Diego Historical Society) interprets the "American Period" of San Diego's history. Below the exhibits floor is housed the Society's Research Archives which contains books, manuscripts, photographs, costumes and artifacts relating to the city's past. The Historical Society, founded in 1928, also operates The Junípero Serra Museum in Presidio Park and the Villa Montezuma (an historic house museum from the 1880s) in Golden Hill. The SAN DIEGO HALL OF CHAMPIONS first opened in the House of Charm in 1961. Its purpose is to honor local athletes who have won national and world renown. Over the years the Hall of Champions has given thousands of trophies, plaques and certificates to athletes. The Hall of Champions exhibits photographs, souvenirs, equipment, mementos, medals and trophies of San Diego's greatest athletes. The SAN DIEGO MODEL RAILROAD CLUB was also originally housed in the House of Charm and continues to be one of the most popular displays in Balboa Park. The hand-made models and layouts resemble to the tiniest detail the nationally known locomotives, sleepers, freight trains and refrigerator cars. It is one of the largest and most elaborate miniature train operations anywhere in the nation. The MUSEUM OF PHOTOGRAPHIC ARTS is at present devoted exclusively to photography, film and video and is dedicated to the present and future state of the art. A variety of changing exhibits displays the works of early photographers as well as contemporary ones. One of several regional art conservation centers in the United States, the BALBOA ART CONSERVATION CENTER maintains a highly skilled staff of experts who restore works of art for a number of west coast museums. A small exhibit area and viewing lab allows the general public to observe work in progress. THE COMMITTEE OF 100, largely responsible for much of the continuing restoration of Balboa Park buildings, maintains its offices in the Casa de Balboa.

The San Diego Zoo

Dr. Harry Wegeforth was obsessed by circus animals from the time he was a small boy. During the Panama California Exposition, he and Dr. Paul Wegeforth had been surgeons for the fair. It is said that riding home from the park one day, Dr. Harry said to his brother, "Wouldn't it be wonderful to have a Zoo in San Diego?" The inspiration came upon hearing a lion roar, one of the few wild animals that were

Elephant Pool, San Diego Zoo

displayed in cages at the exposition. And a moment later he said, "I believe I'll build one." It is reported that he went to the newspaper office that night and talked for several hours with a friend there, and through that discussion evolved plans for the beginning of a zoo. This was in 1916. A modest little notice appeared in the local paper asking any who would be interested in starting a zoo in San Diego to join Dr. Wegeforth in a meeting. Five men responded: Dr. Fred Baker, Dr. J.C. Thompson of the U.S.N., AND Mac and Frank Stephens, the latter a local scientist.

Dr. Wegeforth held the office of president of the Zoological Society which he organized, until his death in 1941. He was much more than president. He served as planner, manager, promoter, financial advisor and, during much of the early years, was the sole financial support of the zoo. He traveled at his own expense, bringing back ideas from zoos and from associates with every important collection of animals in existence. His many contacts enabled the procurement of zoological specimens, as well as trees and shrubs. He also developed the Zoo Hospital. He pleaded for permanent quarters for the Zoological Garden, and finally in 1922 the Society was granted about two hundred acres in an area of the Park, which, rough in terrain, was exceedingly difficult to plant and cultivate. It was an obscure area, far from car lines at that time. Three buildings left from the exposition were the first buildings for the San Diego Zoo. One was the International Harvester Exhibit Building. This became the temporary reptile house. Open grottos were built along a canyon for bears, seals, lions and tigers.

The San Diego Zoo at its original location along Park Blvd., 1915

In order that the zoo could begin to be self-supporting, Ellen Browning Scripps gave money to fence the area; thus admission could be charged. Improvements were largely carried by private donations. Later W.P.A. projects were used to build the zoo. Louis J. Gill, as architect, donated his work and Lester Olmsted built much of the early housing for the animals without profit. Other assistance came from A.T. Mercier, president of the Southern Pacific Railroad. He helped by introducing Dr. Wegeforth to his wealthy partners and friends. As a result, Captain Allan Hancock and Fred Lewis led expeditions to obtain new specimens for the zoo.

Dr. Wegeforth was an expert on animal care as well as on methods of display and of zoo architecture. His ideas were different from the old method of close confinement. His arrangements gave the animals a habitat as near to the natural as possible, and at the same time brought the displays close to visitors.

In 1928 the city finally granted $36,000 for operating expenses of the zoo and in 1934, a provision for two cents per one hundred dollars' valuation to be given the zoo was placed in the city charter. This provision was won at the polls after three defeats at previous elections. At each previous trial, the matter had been thrown out because of a technicality. The Zoo now had a measure of security and permanent income.

The Zoological Society was also given responsibility for management of the Zoo, although title to all animals, buildings and equipment was transferred to the city.

Another name which has become endeared to San Diegans from her many years of work with the Zoo as executive secretary is that of Belle J. Benchley. Mrs. Benchley was the daughter of a well known local sheriff, Fred M. Jennings. She was employed by the Zoo in 1927 as bookkeeper; was promoted to head of the staff, and later to the place she held for many years, that of executive secretary, which to most zoos was synonymous with executive director.

Dr. Charles Schroeder was veterinarian of the San Diego Zoo from 1932 to 1937 and from 1939 to 1941. When Mrs. Benchley retired in 1953 he was named director. He is credited with building the zoo into the foremost zoo in the world. "Where Dr. Harry Wegeforth founded the zoo, where Mrs. Belle Benchley . . . put it on the world zoo map, Schroeder has put it all together and made it click."

Today, in the zoo, fences and cages have come down and moats have taken their place. The Children's Zoo, the Skyfari, the moving ramps, the remodelled animal hospital were all accomplished under Schroeder's brilliant leadership. Many others have contributed to the fame of the zoo. Laurence M. Klauber milked rattlers and sent their dried venom to a pharmaceutical firm which developed the anti-venom—so beneficial to mankind. In 1976 K.C. Lint, curator of birds retired after nearly forty years of work with the Zoo. During this time the number of species of birds increased from 40 to 400.

The exhibits and facilities of the zoo are under a continuous program of improvement. These improvements are frequently financed by generous citizens as was the Turtletorium by Colonel and Mrs. Irving Salomon; the Amphibian and Reptile Exhibit honors the late Laurence M. Klauber, long a consulting curator of reptiles, and the Galapagos Tortoise exhibit is in memory of Gordon Gray, for many years a trustee of the board of the Zoological Society. A bequest from the will of Vera Banner, one ever interested in the protection of wild life, enabled the construction of the lemur exhibit. Throughout the zoo grounds are many gifts and memorial plaques.

The Elmer C. Otto Center opened December 1, 1966. This contains office space and a 204-seat auditorium. The building, costing $750,000 came from a bequest of $1,500,000, disclosed in the will of Elmer C. Otto, retired drug manufacturer who lived on a ranch near Alpine. Although he had been a member of a Zoological Society in the east, he was not known to the San Diego group.

The Wegeforth Bowl in the zoo was the first home of what later developed into the San Diego Starlight Opera, and during the summer of 1968, San Diegans again traipsed to the bowl for the summer productions of musical revues. The real use of the bowl is to entertain zoo visitors with animal shows and these are shown several times daily.

Education, as well as conservation and recreation, is a vital aspect of the zoo operation. Every year tens of thousands of students enjoy educational visits to the zoo, either under the guidance of their own teacher or that of the zoo's education staff. A full program of summer classes is offered for school children, who, living in today's cities, may never see a variety of live animals close-up.

The zoo's research program is active and continues to expand. Miss Ellen Browning Scripps, benefactor of many San Diego institutions, provided funds for the zoo's veterinary hospital and initiation of the zoo's research program.

The San Diego Zoo is owned by the people of San Diego. Each animal, building, vehicle or other asset is the property of the city. But management of the San Diego Zoo is entrusted to the Zoological Society of San Diego, a private, non-profit corporation. Twelve trustees from the San Diego community volunteer much

time and effort to oversee the management of the San Diego Zoo and of its "second campus," the new San Diego Wild Animal Park in the San Pasqual Valley.

The highlight of the San Diego Zoo is its Children's Zoo, opened in 1957. Children and young animals see eye-to-eye in this imaginative kids' zoo built to the scale of four-year-olds, but enjoyable to the young at heart of all ages. The Children's Zoo features open moated enclosures, walkthrough bird cages, nursery, and direct-contact areas where children may pet baby animals.

Perhaps the most popular area of all in the Children's Zoo is the glass-fronted nursery, where young primates and other animals are bottle-fed and diapered just like human infants.

Many visitors marvel at the exotic landscaping of the zoo without realizing that all the plantings have been carefully developed over the years—they didn't just happen. Years ago, the zoo's acres were scrub-covered sandy hillsides with few trees. Today, towering eucalyptus and graceful palms, birds-of-paradise and hibiscus cover the zoo, providing a beautiful garden setting for the animal collection, and incidentally, providing some of the animals' diets. The zoo's plantings have been valued in excess of $40,000,000.

*A portion of the
San Diego Zoo today*

Ladies enjoying the park, c. 1918

BALBOA PARK AFTER THE EXPOSITION

Immediately upon America's entrance in the First World War, San Diegans expressed loyalty to this decision of the Government, and the suggestion was made that the city should offer the now empty park buildings of the recent exposition for housing men in training. On April 6th a patriotic dinner was held at the U.S. Grant Hotel in support of the war effort. Admiral W.B. Caperton, Colonel J.B. O'Neill, Mayor Louis J. Wilde and others made speeches. The plan for using the park grounds and buildings was presented and approved. Funds were raised for necessary expenses.

William Kettner, local representative to Congress, was asked to make the offer of the park to the government, and Colonel D.C. Collier was sent to Washington to contact military authorities in regard to the offer. All grounds east of the Plaza de Panama were offered for military use. The exposition buildings were transferred from the Exposition Corporation to the Park Board which consisted at that time of Thomas O'Halloran, Arthur Cosgrove and George W. Marston. T.N. Faulconer was Executive Secretary of the Park Commission.

The conditions under which the Park would be used were worked out by Admiral Caperton, C.H. Davidson and the Park Board. On May 4, the Park Board formally adopted the resolution giving the buildings and grounds to the Navy Department. A request was made for use of the Administration Building and, on May 8, this was granted.

Park Superintendent John Morley, with a large force of men, made structural changes in the buildings at the request of the Navy. The repairs and alterations went on, day and night, at a cost of $30,000, which amount was refunded by the Navy. Within the next few months all of the buildings east of the Plaza were refitted for naval use, and before the end of 1917, 5,000 recruits were receiving training in Balboa Park.

The Naval authorities gave praise in highest terms for the speed and efficiency of John Morley and his electrical foreman, C.S. Harper, for the work of making the buildings ready for military use. A tent hospital was established in the area of the present Natural History Museum and Park Blvd. The San Diego Naval Hospital of today grew from this beginning. In 1919, seventeen acres were deeded to the government to develop the hospital.

Balboa Park afforded the buildings and the space not only for the United States Naval Training Center but also the Naval Air Station occupied the park for a year. Both had their San Diego beginning in Balboa Park. On September 25, 1917, Lieutenant Earl W. Spencer, Jr., twenty-eight year old aviator was assigned to begin a Naval Air Station; to report to the commanding officer in Balboa Park. (His wife, Wallis, would later gain fame as the Duchess of Windsor.) Spencer faced a difficult assignment. The army occupied North Island and used little haste in making room for the navy airmen. Spencer could not secure a foothold there; the naval training center officers were faced with sufficient problems without taking on the training, feeding and housing of the many air recruits pouring into the park. Spencer was able to start mechanical and ground training for the air cadets, but it was June 1918 before the Naval Air Station left Balboa Park.

San Diegans took note of the struggling military operation in their park. Colonel O'Neill granted the use of the International Harvester Building for establishing what was known as an Army-Navy Y.M.C.A. George Marston, president of the city Y.M.C.A. and the General Secretary of the organization Fred D. Fogg began the work of establishing this facility, forerunner of the Armed Services Y.M.C.A. established on Boardway in 1924. Citizens were asked to donate magazines not over thirty days old. Gertrude

Balboa Park used as a Naval Training Camp during World War I

Gilbert worked with the Y.M.C.A. to furnish music for the Sunday morning services held in the organ pavilion, when the 21st Infantry band also played. A branch of the public library was established with a librarian on duty daily from ten to five. More than 1,000 circulating books were provided and twenty-five current magazines. Individuals were asked to bring to the main library, as donations, books of adventure, history and naval matters. The social graces of these young recruits were not neglected by the townspeople. Two truckloads would be taken to the Playgound Community House in La Jolla each night, about half of the young women in La Jolla were asked to help teach them to dance, an art in which they were found lacking.

The Military Leaves

When Balboa Park was vacated by the military after World War I the condition of many of the exposition buildings was such that the city made firm plans to demolish them and to landscape and create formal gardens over the area. But San Diegans rose in protest. $40,000 was raised, and the buildings were repaired and remained.

In 1922 the Balboa Shuffleboard and Bridge Club at Sixth and Redwood was established. The U.S. Naval Hospital in Balboa Park was dedicated; the zoo was moved to its present location and was stocked with animals which had been displayed at the exposition. Works of art left from the art exhibit of the fair led to the establishment of what is now the San Diego Museum of Art. Nature exhibits stimulated the long organized Natural History Society to organize a Museum of Natural History, and the Collection of Mayan exhibits grew into the Museum of Man.

In March, 1922, George Marston made a public appeal for funds to further repair and renovate the exposition buildings. Marston's appeal carried the message, "Cross the bridge and find yourself in another world." Milton A. McRae placed a dollar and cents argument before the people: "On the material side, the Park puts dividends into the pocket of every person who owns property here, or who has business interests." By preserving the park buildings, the value of personal property would be increased. To accomplish this renovation, $23,000 would need to come from the community; labor costs to the extent of $47,000 would be paid for by the government.

In 1922 the city gave the school system seventeen acres of Balboa Park for the Roosevelt Junior High School.

In 1923, Captain J.B. Gay, retired Naval Officer, promoted the construction of a War Memorial Building in Balboa Park. But the American Legion had spent $28,000 on the old exposition building which housed war mementos and which was used for Legion activities, and General J.H. Pendleton, retired and for whom Camp Pendleton was named, actively opposed a change in either name or location.

Adolph Spreckels had one year to live—he died on June 28, 1924—when his brother John, who had made San Diego his home since he was thirty-four in 1887, realized that the Spreckels interests were not popular, and he gave a great dinner at Hotel del Coronado on May 19, 1923.

John D. Spreckels was seventy-years-old and wanted to present his case to the people. One hundred of the most prominent leaders were invited.

When he spoke, he called attention to the capital which he had brought to San Diego. He and his brother had built coal bunkers for fueling of ships: they established the Spreckels Commercial Company; they helped to bring the Santa Fe Railroad to San Diego; he financed the San Diego division and supplied coal for the engines, and this saved the city from being cut off from this important railroad line. When E.S. Babcock was in financial stress while building the Hotel del Coronado, Spreckels went to his rescue, and the brothers helped with the Lower Otay Dam which also needed financing. He began to buy real estate, erect

Making movies in the park, c. 1920

buildings, and invested his funds in a water supply and transportation for city growth. He stated, almost pathetically, that the aim of his life had been that of building up San Diego.

Spreckels' presentation had an immediate reaction. On June 13 at the U.S. Grant Hotel a great dinner was given John Spreckels, and city leaders convinced him, with their many tributes, that his financial backing of San Diego and his provision for city needs, were truly appreciated.

On July 14, 1923, the San Diego Scientific Library, located in the Museum of Man, was dedicated. George W. Marston, speaking on the occasion, said, "Seven years after the Exposition, the California Building has become a temple of Art, History and Science." He expressed appreciation for the individuals and organizations making contributions to the library, among them Mrs. Blanche Vogdes Kendal, the San Diego Natural History Society, the San Diego Museum, the Medical Society and others. He spoke of the beneficence of the late W.W. Whitney whose bequest for library equipment and maintenance would provide permanent support.

In 1925 Marston asked the city council to reconsider the 1908 Nolen Plan for which study of Balboa Park Marston had provided the finances. The council approved the expenditure of $10,000 and Nolen produced the second Nolen Plan. The study urged against further encroachment of the park, and suggested parkway connections between Balboa Park and the Waterfront. It outlined the use of various areas and the landscape design for each area. It plotted new park roads; it proposed the utilization of the northeast section for recreation and outdoor sports. It urged there be no extension of park projects for other than park purposes.

In 1927 the citizens passed a bond issue to implement Nolen's plan. Included for the northeast section was a swimming pool, six tennis courts, a municipal golf course which was completed in 1932. The northeast development was named Morley Field for John Morley, Park Director for twenty-seven years.

On February 27, 1926, the Fine Arts Gallery, a gift of Mr. and Mrs. A.S. Bridges, was dedicated. On June 7, 1926, John D. Spreckels died and a Memorial Service was held in the organ pavilion which he, together with his brother, had built and donated to the city.

This year too, there was a movement to place San Diego State College in Balboa Park, but it was squelched.

In 1931 work was progressing on facilities for Senior Citizen recreation. At Sixth and Date, courts were provided for horse shoe pitching and shuffleboard courts which could hold ninety-four players at one time. The Senior Citizens Club boasted one thousand members. Shuffleboard Courts were also dedicated at Sixth and Redwood in 1931. Winter guests found other recreation in the lawn bowling, chess and checker clubs, and croquet.

Work on the twenty-seven hole golf course and on the tennis courts provided jobs for the unemployed. In 1932 the swimming pool costing $70,000, together with the recreation center, were nearing completion. The $300,000 bond issue for the Nolen Plan was paying off.

The Natural History Museum was built and dedicated January 1, 1933.

In 1934, Belle Benchley of the San Diego Zoo began plans for the Wegeforth Bowl to honor Dr. Harry Wegeforth, the zoo founder; it opened in 1936.

On December 11, 1934, Sacramento public officials visited Balboa Park for ideas and called it the Number One playground in the state.

Park Buildings Are Saved From Demolition

In the spring of 1933, the 1915 exposition buildings showed great wear and tear. The foundations and arcades of the buildings were partially decomposed. The towers and facades leaned forward as though tipsy, and entire sections of cornices and parapets had broken away and lay in the shrubbery at their base.

Just about this time in the downtown plaza a palm tree toppled over killing a little child. The tree had been eaten by termites. The city inspectors were warranted in their concern for public buildings and went on a rampage of inspection. When they reached Balboa Park they were appalled at what was found and decided that restoration was too costly; the buildings were condemned; they must be torn down! But the inspectors had not reckoned with the citizens, and especially one determined and gifted woman.

Gertrude Gilbert had been chairman for the musical programs of the exposition and was a recognized civic leader. At a public meeting, Miss Gilbert likened the plan to raze the buildings to letting a loved one die because it wasn't convenient to raise money to pay the surgeon. She called on David Millan of the Chamber of Commerce to help her save the buildings. Mostly to humor Miss Gilbert, the city reluctantly called on Richard Requa to make another investigation. Demolition was postponed for one week when a report would be given. Mr. Requa called in Walter Trepte, an experienced contractor, and the result was that for one-fourth of the city estimate, the buildings could be made safe and attractive in appearance. The committee was still reluctant to accept this report, but George W. Marston spoke in his gentle, forceful manner and won an affirmative vote.

At this time the Federal Government, through the Reconstruction Finance Corporation, was about to launch a nation-wide work relief program. Jerome Pendleton, local representative, investigated and found that if one-third of the required amount could be raised; the government would take care of the remaining expense.

A large fund-raising committee under the leadership of the Chamber of Commerce was formed. Hundreds of volunteer workers solicited funds, and many benefit entertainments were held for the park restoration. Harry L. Foster led the drive among veterans for donations, and later he devoted full time to the work on the buildings, serving as head of the "Relief Labor Department." After one month of feverish activity, the needed amount was raised. A restoration committee was appointed with W.L. Van Schaick as Chairman, serving with Gertrude Gilbert, Fred L. Annable, John Morley and city officials. Walter Trepte took active charge of the repair work and was responsible for the thorough and efficient manner in which it was done. The citizens had contributed $77,000 and the S.E.R.A. or government agency contributed $300,000 for labor costs for building improvement.

Buildings And Features Added After The Exposition

Following the Panama-California Exposition, the Friends of Art, predecessors of today's San Diego Museum of Art, brought loan and exchange exhibits to a temporary gallery in what is now the south wing of the Museum of Man. At Christmas time this group arranged a beautiful Nativity Scene about the Organ Pavilion. The Christmas Tree Lighting, long seasonal event, was celebrated by a procession led by the gowned choir, singing carols and carrying lighted tapers as they marched from the Plaza de Panama to the organ.

In 1922, Mr. and Mrs. Appleton S. Bridges gave funds for an art gallery for Balboa Park. Mrs. Bridges (Amelia), was a daughter of H.H. Timken of the Timken Roller Bearing Company. Mr. Timken and a son had come to San Diego where they had invested in a large amount of downtown property. Appleton Bridges was President of the Timken Investment Company. The gift of the gallery was made contingent on the city's giving the space and a society organized to manage the gallery. The present location at the north end of the Plaza de Panama was provided. The gallery which had been estimated to cost $40,000 in 1922, actually cost $400,000.

On February 28, 1926 the Fine Arts Gallery, now called the **San Diego Museum of Art**, opened its doors to the public. The gallery designed by William Templeton Johnson and Robert W. Snyder, architect and builder, contained twelve exhibition spaces with some 12,000 feet of floor space. The building is fireproof and earthquake proof. The design of the building is in the plateresque style of the Spanish Renaissance which, in the early part of the Sixteenth Century, produced the noblest architectural monuments in Spain. In Spanish, the word "Platero" means silversmith, and such was the intricate delicacy of the ornaments of the buildings that they seemed almost to have the refinements of the silversmith's art.

The exterior of the gallery is reminiscent of the Spanish originals which were its inspiration, notably an unfinished fragment of rare beauty which forms an entrance facade of the University of Salamanca. The main feature of the facade is a creation highly architectural in form, but fancifully elaborate in its decoration of floral and animal forms, its sculpture and heraldry.

According to an old legend, Saint James was carried to Spain upon a shell. This feature which occurs in diverse forms of Spanish ornament, is used in forming the beautiful arch over the doorway, as the principal decoration of the rich cornice just below the main roof, and for the adornment of niches for sculpture within the building. As the structure was to house works of art, the architects chose to embellish it with statues and bas reliefs of artists; the famous painters of the Spanish Renaissance: Ribera, Velasquez, Murillo, Zurbaran, and El Greco. No one knew when that sculpture was carved, what art treasures the building would house, but today nearly every one of these great painters is represented in the permanent collection.

A new wing was opened in 1966 which was designed by Robert Mosher and Roy Drew. The style is called Romantic Spanish with Moorish overtones in the interior courts, the colonnades, the reflecting pool and the ornamental metal grills. At this time a new auditorium, with seating for 450, also opened. It was the gift of well-known San Diego publisher James S. Copley.

In April, 1974, the Gildred-Parker-Grant Wing, comprised of two large exhibition galleries and new office space, opened with an exhibition of *Monumental Paintings of the 60's.* The expansive galleries allowed for the first time, in the San Diego area, a suitable place to display art works of such large dimensions being produced by contemporary artists.

In 1975, the San Diego Museum of Art celebrated its 50th Anniversary. To mark the occasions, Betty Ford, the First Lady, dedicated The Carl Skinner Memorial Gallery—an Asian Art Court—which allows a more spacious display area for Eastern Arts.

The May S. Marcy Sculpture Court and Garden was opened in August 1972 as a fenced extension of the courtyard. Here is displayed a wide range of contemporary sculpture, permanently placed. By this means the San Diego Museum of Art has been extended and brought into the twentieth century. A majority of these sculptures are the gift of Mr. and Mrs. Norton S. Walbridge.

Frank and May S. Marcy were patrons of the art museum for many years. During World War II when the gallery was used as part of the United States Naval Hospital, they provided private homes for the use and storage of the gallery. Mrs. Marcy served as president of the Fine Arts Society from 1953 to 1956.

The **Statue of El Cid,** recalling a medieval hero and legends of the eleventh century, was created by Anna Hyatt Huntington. El Cid was known for his support of Christianity and for his efforts at driving the Moors out of Spain.

Several of these statues are in existence. The original is in the court of the Hispanic Society in New York City, an organization which was sponsored by the Huntingtons: Archer M. and Anna. There is another El Cid in Seville, Spain as well as the one made in 1927 for Balboa Park. According to a story told by the late Donal Hord, well-known sculptor, the Johnsons and Huntingtons were friends, although the latter had never been in San Diego. Upon seeing the plans for the Fine Arts Gallery, Mr. Huntington was impressed and said, "No Art Gallery should be without a good library, and I'll start it." For good measure he gave the El Cid also. The full name of El Cid was Rodrigo Diaz de Bivar. Mr. Johnson designed the pedestal of Indiana limestone. The statue stands twenty-three feet tall.

On July 5, 1930, at the dedication of the statue, the Spanish Ambassador was chosen for guest speaker. It was a dignified performance, and all went as planned until His Honor, Don Alejandro Padilla y Bell finished his speech, and with a great flourish pulled the string which would reveal to all assembled the statue of El Cid. Then a moan of disappointment rose from the expectant crowd, as the cover snagged on the spear of El Cid. But this moment of frustration was turned to amusement and expressed applause as two little boys climbed the statue by way of stirrups, untangled and released the cover. In 1967, floodlights placed on either side, give a dramatic light effect at night.

It seems altogether fitting that El Cid Campeador, Chivalrous Castillian, scourge of the Moors and hero of a thousand tales, should stand guard over San Diego's park of legends and romances.

At the base of the majestic entry steps to the **Natural History Museum,** stands a golden sun dial. The well worn letters state that this was presented by Joseph Jessop in the year 1908. It was originally installed on the yard of the San Diego Public Library, and when the building was demolished in 1952 to make way for a new library, the sun dial was placed at the Natural History Museum.

The first Natural History Museum location in Balboa Park was in 1917—in the Nevada Building of the Panama-California Exposition. Other temporary quarters were the Foreign Arts Building (House of Hospitality) and the Electric Building. Where the Natural History Museum now stands, was the former Southern Counties Building of the Panama-California Exposition. This building had been converted into the first municipal auditorium.

On November 25, 1925, Fire Chief Louis Almgren and his men were preparing for the annual Fireman's Ball at the Southern Counties

The medieval hero "El Cid"

Building. Shortly before the hour of the great event, the building was a mass of flames, caused by an overheated furnace. Fortunately the merrymakers had not yet assembled for the festivities. In spite of all the firemen could do, the building was a total loss. Six years later, Ellen Browning Scripps contributed $125,000 toward a new building for the Natural History Museum. The present building was dedicated on January 1, 1933, and the San Diego Society of Natural History had a permanent home. The building was designed by W. Templeton Johnson, architect of the San Diego Museum of Art, Junípero Serra Museum and other beautiful buildings.

The Natural History Museum continues as it has through its long and distinguished history, to concentrate research efforts, outstanding programs and more exciting exhibits on the area known as the Southwest Region. This region includes southern California, northern Baja California and when appropriate, extensions of these areas. Museum curators carry on research throughout the world, research which will help us understand what is happening in our own locale, and lead us to greater appreciation of our environment as it changes and adapts to shifts in climate, or industrial development, or other factors.

In the office of the museum director is a picture inscribed:

Ellen Browning Scripps: Beloved Benefactress of many acts for the promotion of Human Welfare and Educational Advancement, whose generosity has made possible the establishment and maintenance of the museum.

Marston Point is located at the south end of Balboa Drive, across from and east of Sixth and Date Streets and a spectacular view it affords of San Diego. To honor George Marston and his ceaseless and unselfish devotion to Balboa park the City Council passed a resolution November 14, 1924 naming this *Marston Point.*

The Flag Pole was provided by the Free and Accepted Masons in San Diego County on June 14, Flag Day, 1927, and is in commemoration of the Adoption of the United States Flag of June 14, 1777. William P. Lodge was the architect. It was rededicated on June 15, 1947.

The **Carousel** in Balboa Park affords much pleasure to children and grownups alike, and when in 1968 it was closed for several months while being renovated and carried to a new location, there were many evidences of disappointment on the part of park visitors, and impatience expressed at the long delay in reopening.

The Carousel was built in 1910 and was first set up in Los Angeles. Later, it was moved to Coronado and used during the days of the famous Tent City. It was brought to Balboa Park in 1922 by a man named Simpson. Clarence Wilcken began working on it in 1924, and was with the Carousel continuously, eventually as owner along with his son and daughter.

Clarence Wilcken died in 1976 at age ninety-three. He contributed much to the happiness of children during his many years with the merry-go-round; he was generous to the handicapped and to special groups of children and they returned his affection.

The Balboa Park Carousel is one of only seven remaining carousels built by the Herschell-Spillman Company that are still operating. Others are in Greenfield Village, Dearborn, Michigan and Tilden Park, Berkeley, California.

The Carousel occasionally reaches the grownups in its appeal; and the newspaper reports social functions "held at the Merry-go-round!"

Marston Point, 1928

*The Balboa Park
Carousel*

*The Natural History
Museum (opposite) c. 1935*

THE CALIFORNIA PACIFIC INTERNATIONAL EXPOSITION

At about the same time the park buildings were restored, Frank Drugan entered the scene. He was a natural promoter and a man of culture and vision. He immediately began advocating a second exposition. He argued that the economy seemed favorable; that people were restless for travel and entertainment, and that the Chicago World's Fair was closing and many exhibitors could be induced to ship displays to San Diego. Westerners, not having visited the Chicago Fair would come to San Diego.

The city now had a population of 188,000. Roy Hegg of the Chamber of Commerce interested tourists in the idea of an exposition, and Frank Belcher, a banker and later president of the exposition, took the lead in promoting the fair.

The plan as formulated, would ask for subscriptions as a loan. The money would be repaid from the profits of the exposition, and the remainder would be used for civic betterment. O.W. Cotton was chairman of the campaign to raise $500,000. He found at first that everyone wanted an exposition, but that few would help finance it. Joseph E. Dryer, former president of the Chamber of Commerce, expressed the opinion that, but for Frank Drugan, there would have been no exposition. But Drugan so influenced public opinion that by July 27, 1934, the Exposition Corporation was inaugurated and financed. Walter Ames was named attorney for the organization and drew up the Articles of Incorporation.

Colonel Copley had said that when the subscribed funds reached $150,000, he would give newspaper support. He later gave $10,000 and the backing of the paper. Baron Long gave $50,000; Wirt Bowman $20,000, the County and City each gave $50,000, and the fund was over-subscribed by $200,000 with 3,300 persons making subscriptions.

On a beautiful Sunday, December 2, 1934, San Diegans by the thousands visited Balboa Park, attracted by the new buildings in preparation for the exposition, by band and organ concerts, by the zoo, by the museums and by the recreation centers. They had a well earned interest in the park; had saved the buildings through their contributions, and were investing in the coming California Pacific International Exposition.

Immediately after July 27, 1934, telegrams were sent around the world with invitations to participate in the exposition, and arrangements were made to use the exhibits from the Century of Progress, now ending in Chicago. Soon after this, President Roosevelt signed a bill authorizing a $350,000 building for Federal exhibits. Richard Requa was chosen architect of the fair. He had great reverence for the 1915 buildings, now rejuvenated by Walter Trepte. In order to carry on the ideas of Goodhue, embodied in these buildings, he turned to the native architecture of the southwest, the Indian Pueblos, as well as to older structures such as those left by the Aztecs and the Mayans in Yucatan and Mexico.

Frank Drugan and (opposite) the 1935 California Pacific International Exposition

Studies by Requa revealed that the fundamental features of our modern styles of architecture had all been employed in the creation of prehistoric buildings through:

1. Similarity in the arrangements of masses and the use of horizontal lines; and
2. The employment of geometric design in ornamentation, and its use in selected spots such as doorways, friezes and parapets.

Therefore, Requa decided to use for the new buildings, to be developed in the southwest section of the park, the Palisades area, a plan which would trace the history of architecture from the prehistoric times down to the modern era.

Architecture, Design And Events

A plaza was designed for the central portion of the Palisades area, and the buildings were arranged to show progression from prehistoric to modern times. On the west side, today's remaining buildings—Conference Building, Recital Hall and Palisades Building, along with the renovated Balboa Park Club, were all reminders of Indian Pueblo architecture. On the east side the Federal Building, Mayan in design, was modeled after the Palace of the Governor of Uxmal, Yucatan, Mexico. The gymnasium next to it demonstrates the close relationship between ancient Maya and the Twenieth Century treatment of masses and ornamentation. The Ford Building at the center of the east and west buildings was designed to show the latest ideas of modern industrial architecture in a California atmosphere.

To represent the humble dwellings of the masses of early people, simple and unpretentious cottages were to be found in two areas—the Spanish Village and the House of Pacific Relations. Ideas for these buildings were the inspiration of Frank Drugan.

There was extensive use of plants and foliage. Thousands of feet of planter boxes were placed for decorative effects along the parapets of new buildings, and potted plants were used profusely. More than 5,000 decorated boxes, terra cotta jars and flower pots were used in and about the buildings and in the gardens. It was one of the greatest botanical displays ever collected; plants were gathered in from all parts of the world. The cactus garden west of the Balboa Park Club was started under the supervision of Kate Sessions. For the new Palisades area, many more large trees were needed than were available from nurseries; some were donated from the yards of townspeople.

From the time of the decision to hold the exposition, July 27, until the scheduled opening, May 29, 1935, there were only about eight months, but the personnel actively engaged in the building of the fair were great team mates; the job of making the exposition was their religion. They worked, ate and slept with it, and in the end the gates opened on time and the tired crew felt it had been a great experience. As many as 8,000 men were employed at one time, working around the clock. The first 1,400 carpenters employed were taken from those working on other W.P.A. projects.

Frank G. Belcher proved to be an outstanding President of the Board. The responsibility of building and completing the show on time belonged to Zack Farmer who had been managing Director of the Olympics in Los Angeles in 1932. J. David Larsen was his assistant, contributing great patience and tact as well as executive ability. The Director of Works was H.O. Davis who had held an important role in the 1915 fair. He was in charge of landscaping and devised the effective outdoor lighting which added greatly to the charm of the evening programs. The late Roland Hoyt worked with Davis as landscape architect.

Gerald Wellington had charge of the Botanical Building during the exposition. At that time an extension to the north gave much more room. A caged area was filled with beautiful yellow canaries.

H.H. Barter was assistant Director of Works, and as such he supervised the construction and the installation of exhibits. His minute care for details was illustrated during the building of the seating for the Ford (Balboa) Bowl. He constructed seats of various styles, difference in tilt of back, or in height of seat. Then he insisted that everyone in the office, including the secretaries, try out these samples. From their reaction he devised the one most comfortable. Those seats held hundreds of thousands of persons through the years. They were replaced in 1981 with 4,324 new seats.

Walter Tupper was Director of Exhibits, and it was he who worked between the demands of the exhibitor and the builder who, following blueprints, would have to be told to enlarge a door—take out a wall—or make any number of other maddening and time-consuming changes.

Another valuable team mate was Juan Larrinaga, an artist of Mexican parentage who had experience in creating movie sets, and who was an expert in solving many knotty problems. One well known illustration was the ingenious design for the lighting fixtures which can be seen in the House of Hospitality. He designed and constructed these with wall board and translucent paper, imitating iron and other metals so faithfully that they deceived experts.

An excellent article by the late Sam Ervine,

*Construction site for
the 1935 exposition*

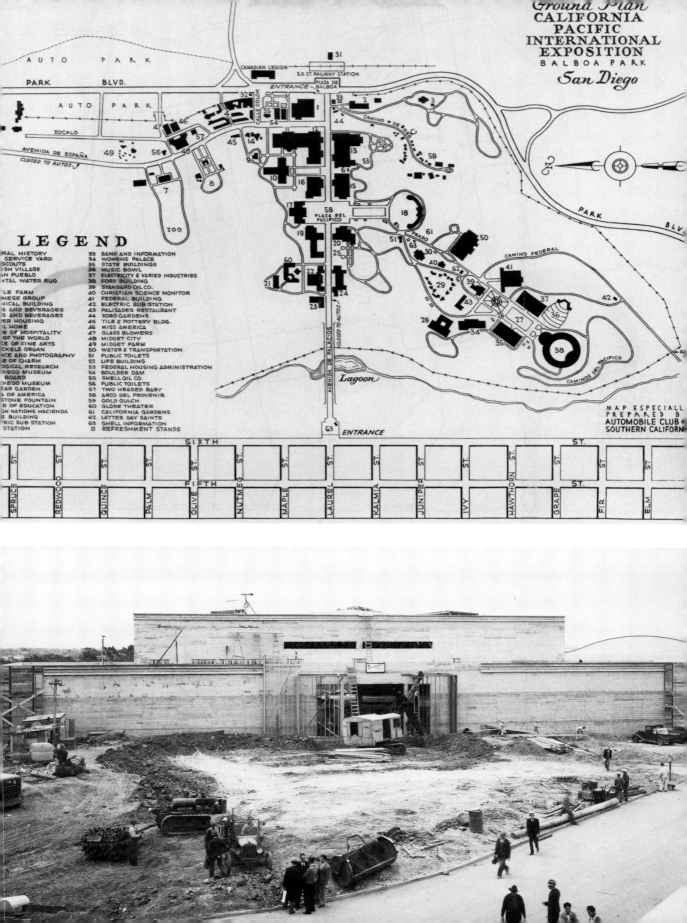

Ground Plan
CALIFORNIA
PACIFIC
INTERNATIONAL
EXPOSITION
BALBOA PARK
San Diego

AUTO PARK

PARK BLVD.

AUTO PARK

Zocalo

AVENIDA DE ESPAÑA
CLOSED TO AUTOS

ZOO

CANADIAN LEGION

S.D.ST. RAILWAY STATION

ENTRANCE

PLAZA DE BALBOA

CALLE COLON

Camino — De Rio

PLAZA DEL PACIFICO

EL PRADO

PARK BLVD.

CAMINO FEDERAL

AVENIDA DE PALACIOS
CLOSED TO AUTOS

Lagoon

CAMINO DEL PACIFICO

MAP ESPECIALL
PREPARED B
AUTOMOBILE CLUB
SOUTHERN CALIFORN

ENTRANCE

LEGEND

RAL HISTORY	33 BANK AND INFORMATION
SERVICE YARD	34 WOMENS PALACE
SCOUTS	35 STATE BUILDINGS
SH VILLAGE	36 MUSIC BOWL
AN PUEBLO	37 ELECTRICITY & VARIED INDUSTRIES
NTAL WATER RUG	38 FORD BUILDING
	39 STANDARD OIL CO.
LE FARM	40 CHRISTIAN SCIENCE MONITOR
NESE GROUP	41 FEDERAL BUILDING
NICAL BUILDING	42 ELECTRIC SUB STATION
S AND BEVERAGES	43 PALISADES RESTAURANT
S AND BEVERAGES	44 ZORO GARDENS
ER HOUSING	45 TILE & POTTERY BLDG.
L HOME	46 MISS AMERICA
E OF HOSPITALITY	47 GLASS BLOWERS
OF THE WORLD	48 MIDGET CITY
E OF FINE ARTS	49 MIDGET FARM
CKELS ORGAN	50 WATER & TRANSPORTATION
CE AND PHOTOGRAPHY	51 PUBLIC TOILETS
E OF CHARM	52 LIFE BUILDING
OGICAL RESEARCH	53 FEDERAL HOUSING ADMINISTRATION
DIEGO MUSEUM	54 BOULDER DAM
BOARD	55 SHELL OIL CO.
KAR GARDEN	56 PUBLIC TOILETS
& DE AMERICA	57 TWO HEADED BABY
STONE FOUNTAIN	58 ARCO DEL PROVENIR
GN NATIONS HACIENDA	59 GOLD GULCH
E OF EDUCATION	60 GLOBE THEATER
S BUILDING	61 CALIFORNIA GARDENS
RIC SUB STATION	62 LATTER DAY SAINTS
STATION	63 SHELL INFORMATION
	☐ REFRESHMENT STANDS

SIXTH ST.

FIFTH ST.

SPRUCE ST. | REDWOOD ST. | QUINCE ST. | PALM ST. | OLIVE ST. | NUTMEG ST. | MAPLE ST. | LAUREL ST. | KALMIA ST. | JUNIPER ST. | IVY ST. | HAWTHORN ST. | GRAPE ST. | FIR ST. | ELM ST.

Plaza del Pacifico, 1935

found in *San Diego Magazine* for June of 1965 describes the 1935 exposition. Mr. Ervine was, on his mother's side, a great grandson of San Diego's Mayor Frary. Sam remembered the fair as a teenager and this gave the article the fresh viewpoint of youth. He said the 1935 exposition was the event which put San Diego on the tourists' calendars.

The Red Letter Day of the exposition was the visit of President Franklin D. Roosevelt. In the car with the President was Frank Belcher in the jump seat, along with Mayor Percy Benbough and Governor Frank Merriam.

The exposition had a tremendous impact on the city. It hit and dispelled the depression doldrums. The fair was the center of the town's social life. As its close social columnist, Eileen Jackson, reminisced about the Loggia Lunch-eons in the House of Hospitality for Mrs. Roosevelt, the brilliant receptions and the delightful Court of Honor Teas.

World famous celebrities came to visit Balboa Park; it was written into film scenarios and in 1935 the U.S. Post Office issued a three cent stamp showing an aerial view of the Exposition. In 1935 the Treasury Department minted 70,132 commemorative half dollars, and in 1936, 30,092 more were issued. The exposition is reported to have cost $20,000,000. It opened May 29, 1935 and closed on November 11, 1935. In all 4,784,811 visitors entered Balboa Park through the gates on Laurel Street. For exposition ground services, college boys were used extensively to man modified rickshaws.

The Chicago Fair Exhibits were outstanding, but the midway was probably the greatest of any fair. At Midget Village was one of the most attractive exhibits. There were also parachute jumps. At the Food and Beverage Building one was given a stick of Beechnut Gum, free samples of Junket, and hot Fischer scones smothered with raspberry jam could be purchased for five cents. There were other goodies about for a hungry teenager. Scattered throughout the grounds were many exhibits of especial interest to young boys.

There was Alpha the Robot who answered questions, got up, sat down, and fired a pistol on command. Sam Ervine later learned that many of these tricks were controlled by an unseen human operator, and he saw his first demonstration of television. A Hum-a-Tune man had an umbrella set up on a street corner with a musical instrument which looked like an aluminum waffle. He peddled trick decks of cards, bird whistles and white mice.

There was an artificial lagoon in front of today's San Diego Museum of Art; Sally Rand performed on a platform with fans and furs; there was Gold Gulch, a facsimile of a gold mining camp; there were donkey rides, a cider mill, and in the Federal Building, they would take your fingerprints if you wished. A large press turned out money; the Forestry Service demonstrated fire fighting techniques each afternoon when smoke bombs were set off over a hill, and in the Ford Building were devices for building and testing cars. Also, there were demonstrations of the "Roads of the World," a meandering affair with inclined cobblestones in one section, and in another a section of the Yuma plank road.

Palisades area, 1935

*Robot
kidnapping
Queen Zorine
of the
nudist colony
1935*

Peepers attempting to view the exposition's nudist colony

There was a big tank where log rollers in huge nailed shoes performed; there was a snake pit with live rattlesnakes in Indian Village; in his midteens, Sam climbed over the Zoro Garden wall and watched the Girlie Shows. He sat through three Sally Rand performances and paid twenty-five cents to see the "Real Gold Gulch Girls."

The exposition was famous for cultural events. It gave impetus to the arts as they are known in San Diego today. The Ford Motor Company brought the San Francisco Symphony, the Los Angeles Philharmonic, the Portland Symphony and the Mormon Tabernacle Choir to perform in the Ford (Balboa) Bowl. In the Ford Building, each day there were music groups performing. Music was coordinated throughout the grounds in such a manner that when no program of music was in progress, recorded music was heard in that area.

The Globe Theatre gave abridged performances four times daily, and oftener on Saturdays and Sundays, of ten Shakespearean plays.

Other expositions have been larger, but the one at San Diego was considered to be the most beautiful. The elaborate night lighting produced spectacular effects. Beyond the Cafe del Rey Moro, one saw the beautifully lighted canyon; there was a romantic log bridge which crossed Palm Canyon near the Organ Pavillion. The Alcazar Gardens seemed to be lighted by 10,000 winking fireflies. There was the Firestone Singing Fountain where the parking lot in the Palisades area is now located. There was the Arc de Triomphe between El Cid and the Fine Arts Gallery. To an unsophisticated teenage boy, it was a Magic Land.

A student pass cost $2.50, a bargain at 1935 prices, with each visit costing 12½ cents. An adult pass was $5.00 and you had your picture on a piece of cardboard.

Many days were designated to honor men and women of distinction. September 22, 1935 was declared "Kate Sessions Day;" she was honored as "Mother of Balboa Park."

The fair was a veritable mecca for musical America. Most of the great artists of the day visited the exposition and gave of themselves to further the "reputation we enjoy as a city of culture." Charles Cadman's visit was the occasion for "Cadman Day" at the fair. Every musical group on the grounds sounded forth in Cadman numbers such as his "Land of the Sky Blue Waters" and his "At Dawning." Madame Schumann-Heink sang at both expositions as did the Salt Lake Tabernacle Choir. The exposition sponsored its own chorus under the direction of Dr. Earl Rosenberg.

The Shell Oil Palace gave travel information with neon tube maps showing the principal highways of the United States. The Standard Oil Palace took the visitor on a tour of the leading National Parks of the west. The Christian Science Monitor, in what is now the United Nations Building, stressed International Good Will.

At the end of the 1935 season, there was $315,833.91 left in the treasury. It was decided to use this to carry the fair over the second year. In 1936, the fair opened February 12. There were 2,004,000 visitors during the year. At the close of the fair there was $44,000 left, which was refunded on a percentage basis.

Emil Klicka set up a booth at Fourth and Broadway to dispose of fifty cent pieces, minted especially for the fair. Some, who bought a supply of these, found that after some years they had become valuable as collectors' items.

Some of the reasons given for the financial deficit of the second year were: competition with a fair at Fort Worth and Dallas, and also many visitors had already seen the exhibits which were sent from Chicago. However, during the two-year period, the tourists, 7,000,000 in number, spent an estimated $30,000,000, and valuable buildings were left in the park.

Water Palace and gardens, 1935

*Cafe in the
House of
Hospitality*

The buildings which resulted from the California Pacific International Exposition and which are in use today are: the United Nations Building, the Balboa Park Gymnasium, the House of Pacific Relations, the Federal Building, the Conference Building, the Palisades Building, the Ford Building, the Balboa Park Bowl, the Globe Theatre, and of course the greatly renovated Balboa Park Club. Considering the great addition to the park and the surging economy, the fair can be recorded as a tremendous success.

On September 9, 1936 the exposition closed. On that day, a parade of floats, one for every state, moved up Broadway at ten o'clock in the morning. The Native Sons of the Golden West presented a float called "The Great Seal of California with Minerva and the Symbolic Bear." The Spanish War Veterans' float paid tribute to Teddy Roosevelt, hero of San Juan Hill. The City of San Diego float presented the first dam in the west, built by the mission padres on the San Diego River. The Navy float showed the historic landing at Old Town in 1846 when they raised the first flag there. The Heaven on Earth Club, founded but lately by Joseph E. Dryer, presented the arrival of Fr. Junípero Serra.

For the afternoon program there were two concerts—one given by the Long Beach Women's Symphony Orchestra and the other by the Bonham Brothers Band. At 10:00 p.m. the model home, Casa de Tempo was awarded to Jorge Almada, son-in-law to President Calles of Mexico. It was estimated that 100,000 persons had paid fifty cents each to view the home; from these ticket stubs the drawing was made. The home had been designed by architect Sam Hamill, as a fair attraction. It was later moved to 1212 Upas Street, where today it stands, beautiful, functional and loved by the owners. An article by Jeannette Branin in the *San Diego Union* of April 1st, 1973 tells the history of the house. At 10:20 p.m., the Long Beach Symphony was heard again. Frank G. Belcher gave the farewell address in which he paid tribute to employees of the exposition.

At 11:30 p.m., Father Time, high on the organ, started closing the World's Largest Book. The 30th Infantry Band gave a fifteen minute concert, and President Belcher presented new Regimental Colors to this military group through Major Stanley F. Griswold. The presentation was followed by a prayer by Dr. Frank Lowe. As the clock neared midnight, a lone bugler on the top of the Palace of Fine Arts sounded Taps. The light on the top of the organ went out as the book closed. This was the signal that the 1936 exposition was officially closed.

On May 28, 1940 the Heaven on Earth Club was officially started to perpetuate the civic impetus inherited from the 1936 exposition. Joseph E. Dryer had come to San Diego to retire. Walking through the exposition grounds he said to himself, "Truly, this is heaven on earth." After conferring with leading citizens, he organized a club by that name. He issued promotional literature, distributed "Million Dollar Sunshine Bonds" and a table showing the relative days of sunshine about the world. This served to advertise and promote San Diego, and in some ways it may be considered to be the forerunner of the now influential San Diego Convention and Visitors' Bureau.

Buildings And Features Remaining From The 1935-36 Exposition

During the exposition, the area now called the **Spanish Village Art Center** was devoted to exquisite little shops, the buildings made to look like a typical Spanish village. Frank Drugan conceived these plans, as he did the House of Pacific Relations. The doorways are deep arched, as are the windows, with antique wooden

Spanish Village Art Center

Old Globe Theatre,
1982

Courtesy, Old Globe

frames. The low roofs are covered with more than 40,000 red tile. The walls were decorated in the colorful flower motifs of the Spanish Renaissance, and plant-filled, vari-colored flower pots lined the window sills and the ledges, and hung from the walls on wrought iron supports. On the east, the deep semi-circled archway and connected tower are capped with overhanging tile, and the tower is surrounded with slot-like windows. The patio is of colored flagstones.

When the fair was over, the village was scheduled for removal, but citizens came to the rescue and asked that the buildings be used as an artists' colony. As a result, the Spanish Village Art Center, Inc. was formed, and occupied the studios until the spring of 1942. The Spanish Village was the only area in the park to be used by the Army during the Second World War. Much damage resulted; the estimate was $13,717.78. The Army offered to settle for $6,453. In addition to the damage under Army use, and before action was taken on the buildings, vandals created great additional destruction. The artist group petitioned for use of the buildings, and after restoration in the amount of $15,000, the group was allowed to resume occupancy and continued with needed repairs.

In all there are thirty-nine cottages, some are used by more than one artist. The kinds of art to be seen are: painting, jewelry, sculpture, weaving, enamel, wood carving, marquetry and photography. The city, by charging a very nominal rent, is in a way subsidizing these skilled artisans. And the San Diego tourists find this a delightful part of the culture afforded by Balboa Park.

One group, which currently occupies a space in the Village, is the SAN DIEGO MINERAL AND GEM SOCIETY, INC. This group's building, at the north edge of the Spanish Village, houses a large meeting room, the walls lined with rock and mineral displays. Another has special grinding and gem or rock working equipment. A third room contains necessary lapidary tools and gas jets for heating metal. There is a concession in the building for lapidary supplies. Jewelry and polished stones are available also.

Visitors are welcome at all times in the Village, and may watch talented and versatile artists at work producing oil paintings, watercolors, sculpture, photographs, ceramics, weaving, gem cutting and heraldry.

An important role in the entertainment during the second exposition was played by the **Old Globe Theatre**. It was a replica of the Elizabethan Globe Theatre, once located on the south bank of the Thames River at Banside, cen-

tral London. The roof cornices of the theatre rose abruptly, and at first were covered so as to simulate the thatched roof. The polygonal shaped main portion and rounded south section followed the design of the original theatre.

During the exposition, the Globe Players were under the direction of Thomas Wood Stevens, world famous Shakespearean authority. Food was sold in the adjoining building known until recently as the Falstaff Tavern; antique style gifts were available in the Old Curiosity Shop, now the office building. After the exposition, many of the buildings were scheduled to be demolished.

The Old Globe Theatre was one of those to be torn down. But in San Diego was a young woman, a sister of Frank G. Belcher, president of the 1935-36 exposition, who had dreamed of a community theatre for this city. Here was a nucleus of one, about to be destroyed. Gathering about her a "Committee to Save the Old Globe" this group began collecting money. They knew there was money provided to restore Balboa Park, after the exposition; the committee observed that the park had never looked better, couldn't some of this money be used for restoring the Old Globe?

Among the many stories of leadership in Balboa Park this account is perhaps the most exciting as one visualizes the "Committee" attempting to forestall the wrecking crew. On the day that Mary Belcher Trapnell—later Mrs. W.G. Farrell—accompanied by a member of her

Lowell Davies, long-time Old Globe board president, is greeted by Queen Elizabeth II on the occasion of her visit to the Old Globe on February 26, 1983.

"Committee" found the much admired fireplace of the Falstaff Tavern completely demolished she begged the wreckers to halt work until she could negotiate with their company. To this the men turned a deaf ear, however she extracted from them the name and address of those she must see. Driving with all possible speed the couple rushed into the wrecking office and asked how they could stop the destruction. Finally when they were given a price, Mary wrote the check from funds collected. The elation and triumph of that moment to Mary and her committee can well be imagined.

The Barn Players who had been organized in 1933, and had been meeting in the old Garrettson estate on Front at Kalmia, took over the Globe Theatre. The group proceeded to make the buildings into a year round type of shelter, and through the years, continuously improved the structures.

On February 3, 1937, the group reorganized and were named the Community Theatre. During the first and second seasons, twenty productions were staged. By 1941, the plant was valued at $35,000.

In 1949, a plan was devised to re-establish the Shakespeare Festival. B. Iden Payne, well known Shakespearean scholar and director, was induced to join the Old Globe to stage *Twelfth Night* for twenty-two performances. He was one of the far-sighted theatre leaders responsible for the establishment of the Old Globe Theatre in San Diego.

In 1968, the Old Globe built a new theatre from the former Falstaff Tavern. This theatre 'in the round' is named the Cassius Carter for the man (1857-1909) who was a noted authority on Shakespeare, a student of languages and possessed a great sense of humor. The new theatre, done in colors of blues, green and gold, affords perfect visibility from every seat and it is a unique addition to the facilities of the Old Globe.

Following a tragic fire, on March 8, 1978, when the original Old Globe Theatre was destroyed, a fund raising effort was begun to build a new theatre—similar to the old one, but with modern improvements and increased seating capacity. This new facility was dedicated on January 5, 1982. At that time the entire Old Globe complex which now includes the Cassius Carter Centre Stage, an outdoor Festival Stage, and the Old Globe Theatre was renamed The Simon Edison Centre for the Performing Arts. This paid honor to a large gift that made possible the rebuilding of the Old Globe.

While the summer Shakespeare Festival is on, all paths lead to the Old Globe Theatre and to this unique sixteenth century English atmosphere. San Diego can proudly boast one of the country's most respected festivals.

Built by the United States Government to house exhibits of many Federal Agencies during the second exposition the **Federal Building** is of Mayan design. Towers rise on either side of the entrance way. The upper portion of these is highly ornamented, and the massive walls rise to an intricate frieze. The main entrance with its triangular shaped window is modeled after the Palace of the Governor, located in the ancient City of Uxmal, Yucatan, Mexico. The glass window originally showed colored figures of a Mayan warrior and slave.

The Federal Building has a seating capacity of 5,000, and an area of 28,864 square feet. Under the present floor is an arrangement for a sloping floor which would make the building usable as an auditorium. At various times the city has considered converting the building for this purpose. But aside from the military occupation during World War II, the Federal Building has served as an adjunct to the Balboa Park Gymnasium, particularly for badminton, and as a location for shows such as the annual Greater San Diego Science Fair, hobby shows, and other similar uses.

The **Balboa Park Gymnasium** was built as the Palace of Electricity and Varied Industries for the 1935-36 exposition. The architecture was designed by Richard Requa to "represent the close relationship between the ancient Mayas and the twentieth century modern treatment of masses and ornamentation or a progression from ancient to modern," as was stated by Requa in his *Inside Lights on the Building of San Diego's Exposition, 1935.*

Following the exposition, the building stood idle until 1939 when it was reopened as the municipal gymnasium. The Navy used the building during the Second World War. In February, 1947, it was reopened for public use after $15,000 had been spent in restoring the building. The hardwood floor is 120 by 288 feet, or 34,560 square feet. There are shower and dressing rooms downstairs; upstairs is an athletic and refreshment shop, loud speaker, and good overhead lighting system. The floor accommodates three full-sized basketball courts, five volleyball courts or volley tennis courts. Five table tennis tables are provided. Bleachers are available for spectators.

The **Balboa Park Bowl** or **Starlight Bowl** was designed by Vern D. Knudson, internationally famous acoustic expert, for the 1935 exposition. It was financed by the Exposition Corporation and the labor was supplied by the W.P.A.

While excavating for the bowl, a fossil was found in an area 170 feet above the present sea level. More than twelve feet of vertebrae column was uncovered in the digging. Clinton G. Abbott of the Natural History Museum identified the animal as having been a denizen of the pliocene period. In life it was about seventy feet long, and was related to a species of the California Gray Whale.

During the fair the bowl was called the Ford Bowl because the Ford Motor Company provided the many symphony orchestras and other free entertainment which performed from its stage. But on April 21, 1948, the name was officially changed to Balboa Park Bowl. The Starlight Opera performances were staged in the bowl in 1948, and by 1950, attendance had grown so that it became necessary to increase the seating capacity from 3800 to 4263. That year a wall was built across the back of the bowl; this improved the sound reception for the upper portion of the outdoor theatre. A movable stage was installed also.

On October 11th 1951, occurred one of the most exciting performances in the use of the Balboa Bowl. The Council of Churches, of which George A. Scott was president, gave the Oratorio Elijah. John Charles Thomas sang the leading role. A chorus of 400 voices came from ninety-one city churches. The San Diego Philharmonic Orchestra played the instrumental accompaniment with Charlotte Dewse at the organ. And Carl Dewse directed the choir, and young Steve Dewse sang a part also. Mr. Thomas had highest praise for the soloists and for the spirit of San Diego.

Summer symphonies and the Starlight Operas became important summer events, and San Diegans looked forward to spending delightful evenings under the stars in the soft air, enjoying the colorful programs of the Starlight Operas, or the popular programs of the San Diego Symphony Orchestra in Balboa Park Bowl. But with 1967 came the decision to abandon the bowl. Air travel had become popular and the flights gained in frequency; the noise was deafening, and the flight pattern was directly over the bowl. That year, both organizations moved to the Civic Theatre or Convention Hall, but to San Diegans, some of the allure was lost by this move indoors.

In 1968, the Summer Symphony moved to State College to an outdoor theater; the Starlight merged with another group and gave two sets of performances at the Wegeforth Bowl at the San Diego Zoo. The bowl had many other uses—the annual piano festival, the celebration of Mexican Independence, recreation programs, and during the summer of 1968 presidential candidates spoke there.

The Balboa Park Bowl (now Starlight Bowl) in the 1930s

In 1975 the Starlight Opera returned to Balboa Bowl. Planes still roar overhead; the performance ''freezes''—resumes in a moment—no one seems to mind. It may be that the plane noise has been somewhat lessened. The Starlight Opera seems to belong in this popular location and San Diegans are delighted at the return ''home.''

The **Ford Building** was built by the Ford Motor Company for exhibits of the second exposition at a cost of $2,000,000. Walter Teague, architect, designed the rounded building to show the latest ideas of an industrial structure in a California setting. Murals on the walls depict transportation varying from the most primitive forms to the rocket planes of the future.

The first year of the exposition, the production of the automobile by means of the assembly line was shown. The second year, the exhibit was called the Palace of Transportation, and all types of conveyance were found here. All kinds of roads were shown, even to a section of the rugged Yuma plank road.

In 1940 the Ford Building was used by the 251st Coastal Artillery. Men were trained in defense and were given technical instruction in subjects such as electricity, radio, meteorology, photography and surveying. During the Second World War in a joint project of the City Schools and the Convair Aircraft Company, now General Dynamics, aircraft employees were given basic training, yet technically it was a Vocational School. The city turned the building back to the park in November 1956 to be used for storage.

Today, the Ford Building is home to the SAN

DIEGO AERO-SPACE MUSEUM and the IN-TERNATIONAL AEROSPACE HALL OF FAME. The Aero-Space Museum attracts thousands of visitors each month with its many impressive exhibits of the history of man's pursuit of flight, while the Hall of Fame honors contributors to aviation and space progress.

The architecture of the **Conference Building**, too, was designed to show the close relationship between ancient Maya and the twentieth century modern treatment of masses and ornamentation, while following the style of the Pueblo Indian Buildings. During the second exposition, it served as a State Building. Later it was used by the National Guard, the Navy, the 251st Coast Artillery, and in 1947, it was restored as the Conference Building.

Until the Convention Center was built in 1964, the Conference Building housed many large meetings. Adequate parking was an advantage for such use, and there was seating for 2300 in the hall. Rooms for smaller groups are provided on the second floor. After the downtown Convention Center was built, the Council approved removal of convention type of meetings in the park, particularly those having to do with commercial exhibits. The Conference Building is widely used by recreation dance groups; and for various types of shows.

The architecture of the **Palisades Building** like that of the Conference Building and the Balboa Park Club, is reminiscent of the Pueblo Buildings of the southwest. Built for the 1935 exposition, it was named, ''The Woman's Palace.'' Before the year was ended, and during the second period of the exposition, it became the ''Palace of Entertainment.'' In 1941, that name was still used.

The offices of the W.P.A. Music Projects were located here. After World War II, the building was restored from Navy funds and was divided into three areas. The city contributed more than $16,000 in furnishing these as the Puppet Theater, The Recital Hall and the Craft Center. The project was completed and the building reopened for use on March 3, 1949. The Puppet Theater is immensely popular with children and the theater serves small stage productions, rehearsals, lectures and film showings. Recital Hall has a seating capacity of 500, a stage with a forty-eight foot proscenium, and dressing rooms. It is widely used by the Recreation Department for dancing classes, rehearsals, and by other groups for conferences, exhibits, flower shows, various entertainments and meetings. The Craft Center has two large rooms, and is used by the Recreation Department for turning out craft projects for city

playgrounds, and by several adult educational groups. Tools and machinery for craft work are provided here.

Frank Drugan, whose initiative largely sparked the second exposition, conceived the idea of a group of small cottages which, among the other types of architecture, would represent the houses, during the Colonial period of Mexico, of the masses—the common people. These fifteen cottages were the result of that plan—and are known today as the **House of Pacific Relations.**

During the exposition, national representatives of countries exhibiting at the fair, mainly those of the Latin American democracies, used the little houses for national headquarters. Each cottage was furnished by the country represented, and was hosted throughout the fair by natives in costumes appropriate to the folk ways of the particular nation. The cottages holding ''Open House'' and displaying the arts and culture of their homelands, proved so popular in attraction and enjoyable to the participants that when the exposition closed, these groups formed a permanent organization which they named the ''House of Pacific Relations.'' The purposes of the organizations are listed as:

1. To bring into closer acquaintance the people of the various national groups represented in its membership, in order

*The Ford Building, 1935
(now the Aerospace
Historical Center)*

House of Pacific Relations, 1935

thereby to foster and cultivate a spirit of understanding, tolerance and good will, and to present to the public the traditions, music and culture of each represented nation.

2. To arrange with the various national groups represented in this membership for the rendition of programs of an educational artistic nature, and which would be beneficial to the individual as well as to the community.

During the Second World War, the cottages were used by the Navy as a club house. On August 2, 1948, at a ceremony attended by 400, they were returned to the former occupants. Melvyn Douglas, screen and stage actor and husband of California Congresswoman Helen Gehagen Douglas, spoke on the occasion. Frank Drugan, founder of the cottages spoke also. Each cottage took some part in the program. William Angus, President of the House of Pacific Relations, received the keys to the cottages from Leo Calland, City Park and Recreation Director. Angus described the organization

as a miniature diplomatic group. He told of the many foreign dignitaries who visit the cottages, and of the hundreds of visitors from other countries who find persons common to their homeland in these cottages. He spoke also of the service of translating letters.

In 1962, the House of Pacific Relations was incorporated under the State of California as a non-profit organization. This unique organization is, so far as known, the only one of its kind in the country, and it draws hundreds of visitors every Sunday to the lawn programs and hospitality of the cottages.

The design of the **United Nations Building** has been called a modification of Spanish Colonial. It was built as the Christian Science Monitor Exhibit for the second exposition. The upper story is set back of the first story level, and is covered with a roof of red tiles, accentuated by overhanging cornices. The building provides five exhibit rooms. In 1938, the "Camera Enthusiasts" secured permission from the City Recreation Department to use the building, and they remained there until 1942

Firestone Fountain, 1935

when the Navy took over most of the park.

In 1948, the building was returned to the Photo Arts Group, and was so occupied until the middle of 1960 when in July, the UNITED NATIONS ASSOCIATION moved into the building.

Balboa Park From The Exposition To The Second World War

On the 30th day of September, 1936, the Federal Building was sold to the City of San Diego for $100, and there were firm plans to convert it into an auditorium. The reason this was never done was due, in part, to more urgent needs elsewhere in the park for the money allotted for this project.

October 3, 1936, the gates of Balboa Park were swung open, and for the first time since before the 1935 exposition, San Diegans by the thousands visited their park without charge. The rehabilitation of the buildings was scheduled to start on the 10th of October and would be financed by an Exposition Trust Fund and by the W.P.A.

January 1, 1937, the City purchased $1,000 worth of electrical equipment and started lighting the California Tower. The permanent lights were turned on in the tower on March 5, 1937 by night and San Diego looked up.

Beginning in 1939 the Park Board abolished parking on Laurel Street.

January 24, the Model Farm Building which was erected for the first exposition and used as his home by John Morley from 1916 until his death, was moved to Navy field where it would serve as an Officers' Club House

On July 23, 1941, it was anno nced that the former California State Building (Conference Building) would be regimental headquarters for the State Guard, and that the Women's Ambulance and Transportation Corps would continue to use the building also.

An archery range was installed at Sixth and Laurel, and the second bowling green was dedicated on June 21 by the San Diego Lawn Bowling Association. An incense cedar was planted in front of Balboa Park Club in memory of John Morley. Tributes were paid by Mrs. Mary Greer of the Floral Association, R.R. McLean, Agriculture Commissioner, Mrs. Bessie Clint, and Park Commissioner Bretz.

In 1941 the City Park Board of Directors were advised to demolish two buildings on Laurel Street, but an architect decided they could be saved for $16,000. Before any action could be taken, the Park was taken over by the Navy for World War II.

California State Building, 1935

THE SECOND WORLD WAR TO MODERN TIMES

The Second World War And The Park

On December 10, 1941, Balboa Park was taken over by the Navy and became a unit of the Navy Hospital. It was named Camp Kidd in honor of Admiral Isaac C. Kidd who died at Pearl Harbor. It became one of the greatest hospital training centers in the world. The wounded from Pearl Harbor were brought directly to San Diego. Rows of bunks were placed in the Museum of Natural History, 960 beds in all, making three times as many beds as the Navy Hospital offered at that time.

In the Museum of Man, most of the exhibits were stored in the basement of the building, and a second floor was built in the rotunda and 759 patient beds were provided in the museum.

The Fine Arts Society was given facilities on Sunset Blvd. where some of its activities were carried on. A total of 423 hospital beds were placed in the Art Gallery. The House of Hospitality became the Nurses Quarters; as many as 600 Navy nurses were stationed there. The Federal Building and the Balboa Park Gymnasium became barracks, housing 1400 men. The Palisades and the Conference Buildings were converted into barracks also. The Balboa Park Club was at first a dispensary, and later became an Officers' Club. It was the last building to be turned back to the city.

The House of Pacific Relations became the Officers' Quarters; the Christian Science Building was the recreation and library center, and the Floral Building was the telephone and press building. The Japanese Tea Garden of the second exposition was a Red Cross Service Men's Club; games of ping pong, cards, and radios were provided, and there were writing rooms available. Women of the Red Cross Canteen Corps served free coffee, punch, cakes and cookies from 3:00 p.m. to 10:00 p.m. daily. Mrs. Ivan Finn served as Chairman of the Red Cross Canteen Service. The old exposition building directly north of the House of Hospitality became a mess hall, and with some enlargement served thousands of meals daily. Meals for 7,000 were prepared in the outdoor galley. The Globe Theatre became a scullery.

In the Ford Building, aircraft trainees received rudimentary training in welding, assembly of parts and allied work. This became, with the cooperation of the city schools, a Trade School. The Balboa Bowl was used by the Navy for lectures and other recreation. The Canadian Legion Building housed the officers and the Electric Building was the discharge center.

By 1944 the former Zoro Gardens area of the exposition had become a Red Cross Recreation Center, and as many as 500 patients daily enjoyed crafts and games there. The lily pond became a swimming pool for hospital patients. This was Balboa Park from 1941 to 1946.

War Ends

On September 2, 1945 World War II ended. As early as 1945, W. Allen Perry, Park Director, was already making plans for planting trees along Park Boulevard from Upas to Laurel Streets; for a fly-casting pool and archery ranges in the Morley Field Area. He reported that in 1944 the Golf Course brought in revenues of $78,212.60.

By September, Leo B. Calland, City Recreation Director, turned in recommendations regarding the use of the buildings. The Palace of Education (Balboa Park Club) would be used for an Events Building; the California State Building (Conference Building) would be used for Drama, Arts and Crafts; the Electric Building for athletic events, and the Federal Building for badminton.

Navy men enjoy the park, 1937

100

On October 1, 1946, the Navy returned the buildings of Balboa Park to the city, and the job of restoration began.

On August 28, 1946 the Council approved the conversion of the Federal Building into an auditorium and appropriated $300,000.00 for the remodeling. However, this work was never done; other financial needs precluded this.

Although the public would be excluded from the park for about a year, on Christmas Day, 1946, the thirty-two-note "Ona May Lowe" Carillon, placed in the California tower, was formally dedicated. It was the largest carillon on the west coast.

On January 2, 1947, it was announced that the buildings would be turned back to the former occupants at the earliest date possible. The City Council objected to the continued use of the (now) Balboa Park Club as an Officers Club. By January 31, El Prado was opened to pedestrian traffic, and three recreational buildings were opened to the public from 9:00 a.m. to 10:30 p.m. daily. The first building to be reconditioned was the Fine Arts Gallery.

The Spanish Village was the one area in the park used by the Army. There was damage to the buildings to the extent of $13,717.78. The army offered to settle for $6,453. Plans for the Palisades (then Hollywood) Building were disclosed to be three in one: a children's theatre (Puppet Theater) on the north end; a Recital Hall with 400 seats in the central portion; the south end would be used for Arts and Crafts by the Recreation Department.

On January 23, 1947 the San Diego claim for restoration of the park buildings in the amount of $840,000 was approved by the Secretary of the Navy, James Forrestal. The amount finally paid was $790,850. However, salvage of war materials netted an additional $13,000. Concrete from war buildings was dumped over cliffs and thus helped to prevent beach erosion.

A special planning consultant, Frederick L. Olmsted was employed by the city in 1947 at a fee of $26,000. He recommended demolishing four buildings. The City Officials had condemned seven, but the citizens spoke out for the buildings and saved them.

In August of 1947, the Park Commission approved the construction of a $300,000 War Memorial Building on the western edge of the Indian Village site.

The question of keeping the buildings seemed never to lie still. In August, 1947, a survey was ordered to determine how many of the condemned buildings could be saved. Meanwhile, Paul A. Wenke and W. Templeton Johnson began the restoration of the House of Hospitality. On April 6, 1948 a committee composed of Paul Wenke, W. Templeton Johnson, Oscar G.

Knecht, Building Inspector for the City, and Lt. Sydney Roppé, Acting Fire Marshall, agreed that only two of the condemned buildings not be approved for restoration.

About this time further park encroachment was threatened, with the City Schools' request to construct an Administration Building within the park. This request was turned down.

One of the most poignant news items gathered from the local paper of that era was a simple announcement, "The Peach Trees are in blossom west of the Cabrillo Bridge." With the problems of erasing the scars of war from the park and the facing of demolition of beloved park buildings—"The Peach Trees are Blooming!" It was almost like reading, "God's in His heaven, all's right with the world."

During 1948 the work of restoration was largely completed. The buildings were assigned, generally, to their functions of today and the Lions Club was granted permission to build a Blind Recreation Center on Upas Street off Park Boulevard.

On the 13th of November, 1948, Balboa Park's newest attraction for youngsters, a forty-eight-passenger **Miniature Train**, made its first run following ceremonies in which a small, but willing, boy drove a golden spike to symbolize the completion of construction. Gary Peeler, three and a half year old son of Mr. and Mrs. Claude A. Peeler of 1502 Acheson Street, was plucked from the crowd and handed a mallet. He laid to with vigor and some assistance from Elwood T. Bailey, member of the Park Commission. The train runs over nearly half mile of track opposite to the entrance of the San Diego Zoo, and is operated under the jurisdiction of the Park Commission by Swope Railways. The city received a percentage of the fares which at first, were: children nine cents and adults thirteen cents.

Leon Bornstein, Vice-President of Swope, spoke at the ceremony. He stated that the locomotive was one-fifth scale of the General Motors F.C. Diesels which pulled the Santa Fe's Super Chief and had air brakes on the coaches as well as the locomotive. To round off the dedication, Miss Mary Meade, introduced as an Eagle-Lion movie starlet, gingerly smashed a bottle of champagne on the cowcatcher.

The Fifties And Sixties— New Directions

In 1953, with the construction of highways through Balboa Park, the charter provision to save land from non-park purposes had to be

Miniature Train, 1954

modified. At the opening of the Electric Show on November 28, 1953, the park was fully illuminated for the first time since World War II. It was stated by the *San Diego Union* of December 18, 1955 that at the close of World War II, $1,100,000 was spent on Balboa Park, most of which came from the Navy. In 1956, a Balboa Park Committee, appointed by the city, drafted a comprehensive report recommending rehabilitation of some and demolishment of others of the park buildings.

Dr. E.L. Hardy, President of State College from 1910 to 1935, became Director of the Museum of Man in 1950, and the Volunteer program was resumed.

The Hall of Champions began in 1958 when on September 28th Bob Breitbard arranged that part of the House of Charm be used for a sports museum.

In 1958 a Balboa Park Citizens Committee took note of the thoroughfare made of Laurel Street and El Prado and recommended the latter be closed to traffic. They also favored a planetarium for the park and a tennis stadium for Morley Field.

A new sound system was installed in the Balboa Park Bowl, thus adding to the pleasure of the Starlight Opera and the Summer Symphony progams.

On September 28, 1958, City Manager George Bean recommended to the City Council that a contract with Harlan Bartholomew and Associates of St. Louis, for the purpose of making a professional study toward a master plan for

Horse back riding in Balboa Park, 1954

Balboa Park be approved. The Council agreed and paid the firm a fee of $35,000 for the study.

On September 29, 1959, Dick Eby, writing for the San Diego *Evening Tribune,* stated that the park buildings had been saved four times, but were now facing another attack. This time the city had paid Bartholomew Associates of St. Louis $35,000 for advice which would have demolished twelve buildings in ten years; but the citizens were ready with advice, for free, and were in a locale where the city fathers were more apt to listen to them than to the experts. In October the City Council expressed strong opposition to tearing down the Ford Building as the planning consultants recommended.

In 1959 there were seventeen miles of bridle paths in the park, and more horses per person in the county than anywhere else in the country. The stable area was leased from the city at $250 per month. The riding club was the largest and oldest in the county, having been founded in 1927 by Mrs. Harry Wegeforth. During the war, one hundred servicemen rode each weekend; hospital patients, fleet personnel, recruits from the Navy and Marines, airmen from North Island and Miramar—all enjoyed riding in Balboa Park. More than one hundred thirty children rode in classes each Saturday morning, with some coming from as far as Los Angeles.

The Balboa Mounted Troop, oldest mounted women's group in the county with a membership of twenty-five participated in parades and horse shows. Of the 125 horses quartered at the stables, forty-five were owned privately.

The preparation for the freeway forced the stables to move out by July 1, 1959. At first it was rumored that a space would be provided in the Morley Field Area, but this never materialized. For the freeway too, many trees would be cut down in the southwest corner of the park. Whatever area was left over would be used by the City Schools for a recreation center and playing field.

In the spring of 1960 a controversy arose concerning religious groups meeting in the park, but the verdict of the Judge ruled in favor of these groups.

On July 8, 1960 the master plan was presented by Harlan Bartholomew, the suggestions covered a fifteen-year period, and a two and one-half million dollar program was recom-mended to rehabilitate the park. Some buildings were to be demolished and new ones built; the park should be closed almost entirely to vehicular traffic; Park Boulevard should be relocated. (This has been done.) New roads were suggested and new pedestrian overpasses and underpasses were recommended. In the first step (1960-1965), five buildings were to be demolished, including the Ford Building. New construction would include two peripheral roads around the park. The second and third stages were also listed in the report. On July 27, 1960, it was reported that the city gave contracts for paths between Laurel and Upas Streets east of Balboa Park Drive, which was compatible with the master plan.

By December, 1960, the City Manager was

Freeway construction in the 1950s changed much of the park

receiving a deluge of protesting letters. They objected to the loss of park land to the freeway, the closing of El Prado, the rearranging of park roads, and the changing of the architecture of the buildings. Many trees of the 1915 exposition were destroyed for the highway interchange; however, the freeway was beautifully landscaped as was promised.

Proponents of park protection had circulated for signatures, a petition to prevent the construction of new roads in the park without the voters' consent, and there were sufficient signatures to place this on the ballot of April 18. However, the Council voted not to place this on the ballot, but rather to submit the question to the City Charter Study Group.

Meanwhile, the initiative petition not to build roads in the park without the consent of the people, qualified for the ballot. The Balboa Park Protective Association were the proponents. The highway department and the Taxpayers Association, plus a new group called, "Vote No on One" were all opponents to the measure, and it failed to pass.

On February 16, 1961, the Senior Citizen Recreation Center at Sixth and Ivy was dedicated. The new Center, costing $112,000 replaced one of thirty years standing, which stood in the path of the freeway.

On June 15 a resolution was adopted to give the schools the eight acres left over from the highway construction. At this time, plans were adopted to demolish the city nursery and to build another at a cost of $115,000. The Council received letters of protest from the Women's Presbyterian Society that liquor was being served in the park at a school for bartenders.

In 1961 the controversy over the Timken Art Gallery arose. The offer to erect the building included a choice of modern Spanish type of architecture. Such dissension arose that the offer was withdrawn. However, the City Council later voted unanimously that the plans offered would be compatible with the park, and the offer was restored.

Controversy and criticism resulted on August 9, 1962, when the City Council entered into contract or lease with a parking concession for a period of one year, which affected three lots east of Balboa Park Bowl. This unpopular city policy was soon abandoned.

In the summer election of 1962, bond issues for Balboa Park and for Mission Bay were turned down by voters. In the City's Capital Improvement Fund of $1,390,000, only $126,000 was earmarked for the park.

On the first Monday of October, 1962, the San Diego Zoo celebrated the forty-sixth anniversary of its founding. Compared to the original membership of forty-one, the member-

ship list had expanded to more than 5,000. On January 1, 1963, the Aero-Space Museum was founded, and opened on February 15, in the Food and Beverage Building.

February 4, 1963, 150 high school and college students, members of Circle K and Key Clubs, conducted one of the biggest clean-up campaigns in park history, during which 200 cubic feet of litter was collected. On November 5, 1963, Clarence (Pop) Wilcken, who had operated the park Carousel for thirty-nine years, celebrated his 80th birthday by giving a party for his friends on the merry-go-round.

In February of 1964 it was announced that fifty eucalyptus trees would be destroyed to build a new wing for the Fine Arts Gallery (now the San Diego Museum of Art). Buildings, long closed from the first exposition, were removed at this time, which resulted in a much better view of the California Tower. The Fine Arts Gallery presented the city a check for $530,000 to be used for the new wing. Previously the gallery had spent $74,000 for preliminary expenses. The addition would cost $1,543,000, and an arcade was planned to join the area between the Fine Arts Gallery and the Timken Gallery.

On January 20, 1966, the *San Diego Union* stated: Of the $23,800,000 bond issue voted for parks, $7,340,000 would be used for Balboa Park. In February, a contract for $474,616 was awarded to the R.E. Hazard Company to relocate Park Boulevard east of the former street. This would add flat land to the west side of the street for park use and for Zoo parking. Early in June 1966, $2,521 was spent for a new awning for Balboa Park Bowl. By the next summer, 1967, the Starlight Opera and the San Diego Symphony had abandoned the park because of the deafening and disturbing airplane noise, and had moved to Civic Center.

In 1966 the San Diego Botanical Garden Foundation, Incorporated, was organized to finance and develop a garden center in the park.

On July 12, 1966, the John S. Alessio family presented a gift to the city to provide lighting of the California Tower. Now, with quartz iodine lamps of 48,000,000 candle power shining on it, the beautiful tower is visible for many miles.

The Cafe Del Rey Moro in the House of Hospitality has for many years been a beautifully appointed and deservedly popular restaurant. With the ball room and other private rooms nearby the restaurant can handle several parties at the same time. Weddings are often held in the garden of the Cafe and receptions very frequently in the different rooms. The patio dining area shaded by canopy and umbrella is an especially attractive place to eat. A cocktail lounge and liquor service add enjoyment for many visitors.

A splendid restaurant in the zoo and two concessions are available.

Portable food dispensers are used in various parts of the park as need requires.

Yet many Sunday visitors ask, "Where can we find a good breakfast?"

The $59,654 contract for the new club house at Morley Field was awarded in September, 1966 to the Haddad Construction Company. The Club House was finished in 1968. The Pepper Grove Picnic Area received a substantial gift from the Thursday Club which provided for new play equipment and the development of an extended area for the children's pleasure. This was arranged through the Park and Recreation Department on January 29, 1967.

In February, 1967 the City Council gave informal approval to an amendment of the city's Balboa Park Use Policy which would discontinue conventions and bar commercial exhibits in the park. This was recommended by the Park Board.

Dave Roberts, assistant Park Superintendent, was credited with the statement that the 21,640 trees planted for the 1915 fair were too many, and that although they compete with one another, no one wants any cut down.

In November, 1967, Colonel Irving Salomon donated playground equipment to the extent of $3,500 for a shady area north of the Redwood Club location. New restrooms were built in this area with attention being given to child size fixtures. But nearby, space was taken from the park for additional parking, and this caused considerable criticism.

Almost the last business of the City Council in 1967 encouraged the efforts of "The Committee of 100" who had struggled valiantly for a commitment on the style of architecture for future park buildings. The City Park Board adopted the policy of Spanish colonial for all buildings along the Prado and the City Council concurred.

In February, 1968 the Balboa Park Carousel was moved back to its first location—a block north and near Park Boulevard. After extensive repairs and a new housing, it was finally reopened on August 6. Six months without the merry-go-round seemed a hard trial for many little people who sought information repeatedly on when they might ride again. In June, 1968 the City Council gave Mrs. Virginia Long and "Pop" Wilcken a ten-year lease to operate the Carousel and a Kiddie Airplane ride in Balboa Park.

On April 10, 1968, following a moderately severe earthquake, the Food and Beverage Building along the Prado was closed and declared unsafe for public use. At last the vital question must be answered—what to do about the building. For a time there were some who thought it could be repaired and saved, while others were in favor of dressing up the exterior to last over the approaching 200th Anniversary of the City, and then demolishing it. Finally the question was resolved when the city sold the

The San Diego Museum of Art as viewed from the Timken Gallery, 1967

building to a wrecking company for $25.00. By the end of December 1968, it was carefully taken apart. The Mayor of San Diego suggested that a bond issue be put on the November ballot to provide funds for a new building, and there was an enthusiastic affirmative vote for this.

In order to perpetuate the beauty of the former building, a concerned restoration group called the Committee of 100 undertook the removal of much of the statuary that this might be reproduced for the new building. Fund raising events helped finance this costly procedure. The now beautiful Casa del Prado attains added significance from this community participation under the leadership of the dedicated Committee.

On May 27, the men and officers of the *U.S.S. Constellation* presented a Memorial Sun Dial to Balboa Park. It was placed in the north lily pond at the Botanical Garden, and was dedicated with proper military ceremony. One like it was to be presented to San Diego's sister city, Yokohama, Japan, as a tribute to the understanding and good will existing between these two cities. As the *Constellation* visits Yokohama or returns to its home port, San Diego, the Sun Dial will represent the constant vigil that this "Ship of the Stars" maintains on the Pacific waters linking these sister cities.

On June 15, the City Council accepted fifteen pieces of play equipment valued at $5,000 from Col. Irving and Mrs. Salomon. The Council adopted a resolution saluting Salomon for his repeated acts of civic generosity, as a similar gift had been received in 1967. A life long interest in children prompted these colorful additions to the park. Col. Salomon, a retired manufacturer who came here from Indiana, formerly supported a boys' camp in the east. In San Diego he continued to serve on boards and committees of many cultural and charitable organizations; his generous gifts have enriched our city.

In the Palisades area a playground for the handicapped was installed west of the Conference Building in 1976. This was a gift to the city from the Kearny Mesa Rotary Club from a $17,000 Art Pratt Memorial Fund. Equipment and facilities are especially designed for the handicapped. Their needs have also been provided for in the park by wide marked parking places and ramps to ease travel by chair or crutch.

The archers of Cabrillo Canyon now have convenient rest rooms and an equipment center south of the Alcazar Garden.

In the Morley Field area many improvements have been made. New trees were planted, tables and benches are in shady areas or placed with a view of the city or recreational events considered. On newly filled park ground shrubs or trees which add nutrients to the soil are chosen.

Altogether it would seem that the park development and maintenance is well administered.

The Park and Recreation Department of the city carry on hundreds of activities every week; these programs are posted on various bulletin boards in the park and may be found in the local papers.

Another Marston Gift To Balboa Park

On May 7, 1976 Mary Marston, daughter of George Marston, gave the beautiful family home designed by Irving Gill, to become a part of Balboa Park at her death. It has been designated for use by the San Diego Historical Society.

This choice 4:5 acres will be the second addition of acreage from the Marston family. The first occurred in 1925 when on May 10th Mr. Marston deeded 15:85 acres known as Marston Hills Addition to the city to be added to the park.

On April 2, 1925 George Marston wrote to the *San Diego Union:*

"Balboa Park is primarily a park to be cherished as a place of natural beauty. Although it is one of the largest parks in the country the time is coming when the building of hospitals and schoolhouses or even libraries and museums must cease or else we shall have a city there instead of a park."

Mary Marston

The George White Marston Home

Arbor Day (Tu B'shvat) January, 1973

The first celebration of Arbor Day in Balboa Park, occurred March 17, 1904. Then the park was called only "City Park."

In 1973, on two successive days, January 13th and 14th, the Jewish Arbor Day TU B'SHVAT, combined in Balboa Park a beautiful religious celebration, together with the addition of about 250 new plants and trees to replace those destroyed by a recent fire.

On September 27, 1972, the Fire Department was called to battle fire of incendiary origin, which destroyed trees and native shrubs on a hillside called Nate's Point. This is located due west of the Balboa Park Club and across the freeway.

Officials of Temple Beth Israel School of Religion seized this incident of wanton destruction of plants, as a civic need on which to focus an annual religious observance. The Park and Recreation Department was consulted and responded with complete cooperation.

As a preparatory measure, irrigation was installed in the burned area; a design was drawn for placing the new trees and shrubs, and these were made ready from the city nursery. The Temple Beth Israel School director repeatedly praised Ralph Carrizosa of the park staff, who gave his Saturday and Sunday to help with the planting.

Each day about a hundred children and adults went marching, singing and chanting from the school at Third and Laurel Streets to the gardener's building at the southwest side of Cabrillo Bridge. Here each child selected a plant or shovel, made ready by Mr. Carrizosa and continued the trek to the burned area. There they tenderly placed new shrubs and new trees to repair the recent destruction. They replaced plants of eucalyptus, Spanish broom, wild cherry and rhus. These were the types which had been destroyed.

This religious celebration of young life and of spring was filled with beautiful verses, several written by the students:

"On this Tub'shvat, this New Year of the

Arbor Day, January 1973

*A great variety of trees
now flourish in Balboa Park*

trees, each of us will replenish the earth. We will place into the ground, something maturing as we are maturing. We will care for their roots; we will give them nourishment; we will help them to begin the season of their freedom.''

Additions Since The Second Exposition

On the front wall of the California Tower is a brass plaque on which is inscribed:

Ona May Lowe
Carillon
given
In her Honor
By her Son
Frank M. Lowe Jr.
Christmas 1946
and
Commemorating the Peace
September 2, 1945
Replaced in her Memory
Christmas 1966
With a
100 Bell Symphonic Carillon
Dedicated April 30, 1967

The park had been closed to the public nearly five years during the War years, but on Christmas Day, 1946, it was reopened with a beautiful community program celebrating the gift of a **Carillon** to Balboa Park.

The Dedicatory Program for the chimes, originally planned for the Plaza de California, was moved into the Globe Theatre when it began to rain. At this time Harley E. Knox was Mayor, Fred Rhodes was City Manager; the Councilmen were Walter Austin, Elmer H. Blase, Ernest J. Ford, Gerald C. Crary, Charles C. Dail and Charles B. Wincote. The Park Commissioners were Milton P. Sessions, President; Howard B. Bard, Roland S. Hoyt, and the Park Director, W. Allen Perry.

The services began at one o'clock on that Christmas Day of 1946. The people of San Diego, shut from the park for five years by the ugliness of war, gathered for the beauty of music and to hear a new means of expressing it at the season most symbolic of love and peace. Dr. Bard of the Unitarian Church presided during the first part of the service. The audience, led by the Community Chorus, sang "America." Dr. Roy Campbell gave the Invocation; Carl Dewse directed the Community Choir, and his wife, Charlotte, played the organ.

Dr. Frank Lowe came to San Diego on January 1, 1934, on a vacation trip and stayed to make this his home and to give many years of continuous service to the community.

Dr. Lowe has been an active participant in almost every civic enterprise. He first served as a pastor; after five years he served as Head of a Christian Institute. He broadcast on Sundays from "The People's Radio Pulpit" for twenty-eight years. He conducted Sunday morning services at the Armed Services Y.M.C.A. for more than twenty years. He has served as Chairman of the Park and Recreation Commission, the Family Welfare Association, the County Chapter of the American Red Cross, the U.S.O. Advisory Council, and the County School Board Association. For ten years he served as a member of the San Diego Unified School Board, and was President for three years.

Dr. Lowe has been sought for hundreds of ministerial functions, and it was he who closed the second exposition in 1936. His explanation for these years of service was modestly expressed when, at a great civic luncheon honoring him as community, educational, and civic leader he said, "I guess I never learned to say 'No.' " And so, in beautiful Balboa Park, and in the spectacular California Tower was dedicated the Chimes which memorialized a "deep longing for peace."

On Christmas, 1966, Dr. Lowe presented a new set of 100 chimes to Balboa Park. These were dedicated on April 30, 1967. His mother, in whose honor the first chimes were dedicated, had died in 1959, and these were given in her memory.

The *San Diego Union* noted: "The carillon in Balboa Park has no bells; it consists of a two-tiered keyboard like an organ with wires attached to what looks like three giant fuse boxes in the wall. Inside each are L-shaped wires of varying lengths that look slightly larger than a coat hanger, dangling from nylon strings. They are made from the same material as bells, a mixture of bronze, copper and other metal alloys. The electric impulse activates the little hammer armature which bangs against the metal and causes the reverberating tone. Each metal string is equipped with its own microphone. The Carillon never goes out of tune."

Paul Peery, retired Army Officer, was Carilloneur while at West Point where he graduated in 1928. He has played the chimes in Balboa Park from the first installation on Christmas, 1946, and is the author of "Chimes and Electric Carillons," a textbook on the instrument. He died on November 15, 1941.

The Carillon's bright chimes ringing out from the California Tower provide an appropriate tonal and musical complement to great architectural beauty. Surely the gift from Dr. Lowe is one of the finest of the many contributions to the park.

On August 21, 1947, the Park Commission approved the construction of a $300,000

The Balboa Park Carillon is in the tower of the California Building

110

Veterans' War Memorial Building on the western edge of the former Indian Village site, north of the Zoo. The building is of low, modern design, surrounded by extensive lawns. It was built with funds from the sale of lumber at Camp Callan barracks, and an arrangement between the government and the city. It was furnished with $18,500, a trust fund which came from the "Buddy Beds" operation. So it cost San Diego nothing.

The War Memorial Building is operated by the incorporated body of the same name, and is used by Veterans' groups for meetings, conventions and social events. Provided are six meeting halls, each with an area of thirty by forty feet, and a seating capacity of one hundred; and an auditorium with a stage. This room is sixty by sixty feet and will seat five hundred. Also provided is a large, well furnished kitchen and a small Conference Room.

The story of the **Timken Art Gallery** goes back in San Diego history to 1926. Mr. and Mrs. Appleton S. Bridges, residents of Point Loma, presented the building called the Fine Arts Gallery, now the San Diego Museum of Art, to the City of San Diego in that year. Mrs. Bridges, the daughter of Henry Timken, subsidized the Fine Arts Gallery during her lifetime, paying the director's salary, and those of the guards. As needs arose, she provided additional funds. When Mrs. Bridges died in 1939, the Putnam sisters, Annie and Amy, assumed the responsibility for the support of the Fine Arts Gallery. In addition to maintaining the gallery, the two sisters began to purchase important paintings for it. The Putnam sisters never married, and as they grew older, they decided to make their estates available for future purchases of paintings. In 1950, the Putnam Foundation was formed, with Walter Ames as its president.

An attorney of long standing in San Diego, Mr. Ames' association with the art complex in Balboa Park goes back to 1926, as Mrs. Bridges' legal advisor. Mr. Ames was also a friend and counselor of the Putnam sisters, and it was he who organized the foundation for the two Putnam ladies. With his guidance, Annie and Amy Putnam commenced to search for fine paintings by the old masters. Within a few years, they had purchased several paintings, among which were ones by Petrus Christus and Peter Brueghel, the elder. The Foundation elected, for a number of years, to loan these paintings to the National Gallery in Washington, D.C., and the Metropolitan Museum in New York City.

On a business trip to Canton, Ohio, Mr. Ames visited the homes of his friends and clients, Henry and Robert Timken. Through Mr. Ames' influence and with his suggestions, the two brothers became interested in building a gallery

in San Diego to house the growing collection owned by the Putnam Foundation. Mr. Ames obtained permission from the donors to call the new gallery, the Timken Art Gallery. The Gallery would house the paintings purchased by the Putnam Foundation and a few of the Putnam paintings on loan from the Fine Arts Gallery.

Mr. Ames and the Board of Directors set about the arduous task of planning the new gallery. Their goals were high. It was their aim to display the Old Masters in as near perfect condition as possible. Two very important factors received special attention. One was the atmosphere in which the paintings were to reside. The other was the matter of security and safety provided for the paintings. Mr. Ames and the architect, Mr. Frank Hope, spent many months traveling and investigating other galleries to obtain outstanding specialists in every field of construction.

The Timken Art Gallery is constructed entirely of travertine marble imported from Italy. Large bronze doors protect the main galleries. The design of the building is low, compact and contemporary. It is composed of two wings connected by a glass hallway which provides the visitor with a view of a small garden of flowers, rocks and weeping pear trees.

There were four interior galleries that house French, Flemish, Spanish and Italian paintings. In addition to this collection, one gallery was set aside to house Miss Amy's private collection of Icons. The wall covering in this room is a fine Italian velvet woven expressly for the Timken Gallery by an Italian craftsman in Florence. The Gallery opened its doors to the public in October of 1965.

A huge water tank, built during the second world war, as an auxiliary water supply for the Navy Hospital, has become a unique center for Spanish American citizens to further the arts and crafts of their heritage and is called the **Centro Cultural De La Raza**.

This movement began with a few Chicano artists and has developed into one of the few such centers in the entire country. At first a group calling themselves the Artistas del Barrio persuaded the Park and Recreation Department to allow them the use of the Ford Building. Here they practiced arts and crafts and music, ballet and folk dancing were introduced as part of the activities. In 1970, however, other use was hopefully planned for the Ford Building. The Chicano group were persuaded to use the north water tank in the Pepper Grove area. They moved in during May, the dedication was July 11, 1971.

Workshops in the various artist and craft media have been established. The exterior of the building has been decorated by the organization.

On November 14, 1971, the **Casa del Prado**

The Food and Beverage Building before being rebuilt as the Casa de Prado in 1968

was dedicated. Ferdinand Fletcher was master of ceremonies at the colorful event which took place in the south patio. The Marine Band, in blue uniforms, played from the loggia above the west archways. Flowers were everywhere. Great clusters of balloons gave vivid accents; some were anchored to a temporary rostrum; others were held by individuals. The invocation was most appropriately pronounced by Dr. Frank Lowe, of nearly forty years service to our city. He said, "Gracious God, we pause a moment to honor Thee—to listen to the still small voice of Thy Invisible Presence. For Thou art indeed spirit, and dwelleth not in temples made with hands, however, Dear Father, today we dedicate one made, wonderfully made, with hands; planned with human knowledge; and ceaselessly promoted by a tireless Committee, stout-hearted, civic-minded. Thanks to Thy divine Providence for this successful teamwork, this beautiful addition to Beautiful Balboa; this brand new light and shining light for El Prado; this united enterprise in which the whole city, official and otherwise, takes great pride. Grant, Dear God, that

the wholesome, youthful use of this palatial 'House by the Side of the Road'' may always prove worthy of such a grand beginning, is our prayer, in spirit and in truth, Amen.''

Dr. Walter Anderson of the National Endowment For the Arts, Washington, D.C. was the speaker. Mayor Frank Curran presented the building to the citizens. Mrs. Frank Evenson accepted on behalf of the citizens. Carleton Winslow Jr., son of the original architect, was an honored guest.

Casa Del Prado provides an exciting chapter in the history of Balboa Park and for a beginning, reference must cite the "tireless committee, stouthearted, civic-minded" of the dedicatory prayer. That committee, organized in 1967 by Mrs. Frank (Bea) Evenson for the preservation of Spanish Colonial architecture in Balboa Park was named by the eminent architect, Sam Hamill, "The Committee of 100." Soon there were more than 1,000 members.

Mrs. Evenson began as a citizen, unskilled in political maneuvering. She saw a need for saving a stretch of beach along San Diego Bay

Bea Evenson, 1971

for a park. She began, singlehanded, to work
for this; she organized a committee who shared
her views. The result was the beautifully landscaped area of Harbor Drive dedicated January
10, 1968. On May 8th, 1976, in this area, the
Spanish Landing monument was dedicated.

The completion of the Casa Del Prado is due
in large part to the tireless efforts of Mrs.
Evenson and the Committee of 100. Her prototype in park history must surely be Gertrude
Gilbert of forty years earlier.

As was noted previously, ornamentation was
removed from the old Food and Beverage
Building, a part of the 1915 fair, and stored for
recasting, which would embellish the new
building. Bonds for the Casa del Prado were
voted in 1968. The "Committee" raised $75,000
of the $96,000 needed for the project, raising all
of nearly $100,000 toward the building by San
Diegans.

Architect Sam Hamill acted as consultant for
the Casa Del Prado. As a boy of twelve, during
the Panama-California Exposition he acquired
a love and appreciation for Spanish Colonial
Architecture, and this influenced his choice of a
profession. He designed the renovation of the
House of Hospitality, the Southern California
Exposition Halls, and he was supervising architect for the Community Concourse. Richard
George Wheeler, Casa Del Prado architect, had
long been acquainted with Spanish Colonial Architecture. As a boy of seventeen, his architect

**Architectural elements from
the Casa del Prado**

father assigned to him the sketching of the 1915 Panama-California Exposition buildings. The Nielson Construction Company was awarded the $2,900,000 contract for building the Casa Del Prado.

The restoration and casting of the ornaments was done by the Ninteman firm. Vincent, John, Burt, and Richard Ninteman all worked on the Casa Del Prado. This firm had done similar work on the University of San Diego and on the restoration of the San Francisco 1915 Palace of Fine Arts. Christian Mueller, specialist in ornamental casting, and five other model makers were part of the Ninteman team. Mueller, too, had played a major role on the Palace of Fine Arts restoration. He stated that he came full circle in his craft since, years ago, he had worked to create the decorations which he now restored.

The visit of Carleton Winslow, Jr., son of the architect who designed the original building in 1914, is the final nostalgic thread, binding Casa Del Prado to a yesterday. Winslow said his father came out from New York and lived near Sixth Avenue. There was no Cabrillo Bridge and he walked the canyon every day. His father designed the "Mary Star of the Sea" church in La Jolla, and the tower and chapel of the Bishop's School in La Jolla. Winslow, Jr., consultant for the cultural Heritage Board of Los Angeles, said, "I've worked with many committees but I've never seen one as dedicated as the Committee of 100."

Casa Del Prado is designed, basically in two sections, connected by an arcade and a large court yard. The northern section of the building, fronting on Village Place, contains 9600 square feet, 1500 seat auditorium. There is an 80 by 35 foot stage; a 10 by 40 foot orchestra pit. Two storage rooms, five practice rooms, dressing and rest rooms, a foyer and ticket booths are provided. Special treatment in the auditorium gives excellent acoustical control; stage lighting may be operated from the rear sound and projection room or from the stage. The building is designed as a multi-purpose facility for youths and adults.

A plaque on the northeast corner of the building states: "Dedicated to the Citizens of San Diego, and the Committee of 100, whose vision made this building a reality." Following are the names of the city mayor, council members of 1968 and 1971, the city manager, city attorney and special project director.

Casa Del Prado is a permanent restoration of reinforced concrete. Its predecessor, the Food and Beverage Building, was the largest, and considered the most beautiful of the Panama-California Exposition buildings. It was designed by Carleton Winslow and built by Frank P. Allen, Jr. The statuary work was by H.L.

Schmohl. The little chapels of the great cathedral in Mexico City were said to have suggested the design. It served first as an exhibit hall for Varied Industries in 1915. In 1916 it was used for Foreign and Domestic Products. The Navy used it during the First World War. It was later the County Fair Building, during the Second World War it was part of the navy hospital, afterward, when restored it served many groups and activities.

Barbara Jones, in a description of the building, notes: "On the new building are elaborate embellishments of plant design such as grape vines, acanthus leaves, grape and olive leaves, fruits and seeds. Neptune faces, the Roman God of the Sea, are fitted into these decorations. The El Prado side, which is completely restored, is adapted from the patio of St. Augustine of Querétaro, Mexico. The auditorium front is in the style of a Spanish-Colonial church. St. Jerome, translator of the Bible into Latin in the 4th Century, is over the door. Classical Cherubs (celestial spirits) are in the design above, and angel faces are on four sides of the columns on each side of the rose window. The large facade over the building name is centered with a statue of the Goddess of California with an Indian and Spanish child. To the right is Queen Isabella and to the left is a figure symbolic of all Anglo-Saxon women. The figure at the top symbolizes universal religion. The ornamental shields on the corner pavilions are of a ship coming through the locks of the Panama canal and of Father Serra. The scallop shells depict St. James (Santiago)".

Alice Mary Greer, writing in *California Garden* for their 50th Anniversary number said that on visiting garden shows on her trip abroad, she came back to San Diego wishing to organize one here, and promoted it through the local Chamber of Commerce. Her notes of the first meeting held in the express office, on Broadway, in June 1907 were kept, as she wrote, on a scrap of paper. But a **San Diego Floral Association** was organized and Alfred Robinson is given credit for founding it. For a time they met in his home, where the Rosecroft Gardens are now located. At the first meeting she mentioned Reverend Hinson, Fred Carpenter, and Louis Blochman. The purpose of the society was stated:

"To promote the knowledge of Floriculture, to Stimulate the beautifying of San Diego Gardens, to hold flower shows, to conserve wild plant life, and such other matters as pertain to such an organization."

Later the Floral Association was given room in the old Chamber of Commerce Building, in 1923 they were given the old Utah Building of the first exposition, where they were, until after the Second World War, returning when the buildings were renovated after the war. In 1971 they were given headquarters in beautiful Casa Del Prado.

California Garden, oldest such magazine in the United States, in continuous publication, was started in 1909. Many garden clubs as well as those in some way associated with the San Diego Floral Association, are listed in the back of California Garden.

The Floral Association has been of great service as a civic aid, especially during both expositions when members contributed greatly from private gardens and resources to help make the fairs outstanding as "garden fairs."

At five o'clock, on the evening of October 20th, 1972, acting Mayor Floyd Morrow and San Diego's "Mr. Water," Fred Heilbron, together pulled a switch and started the city's highest fountain. This is located in the newly created **Plaza de Balboa**. The beautiful fountain is located in what was formerly the intersection of El Prado and Park Boulevard. The pool is ringed by a 200 foot wide concrete base. The main stream of the fountain soars 50 to 60 feet

in the air, other sprays are directed from the surrounding ring toward the center.

When the wind blows harder than usual, a wind-sensing device will cut the volume of water, to avoid soaking the surrounding plaza. The fountain pumps 2100 gallons of water each minute, 1400 of these to the main center spray. The pool holds more than 25,000 gallons. The plaza project inlcuded also a foot bridge over Park Boulevard.

Near the fountain is a park bench dedicated to Bea Evenson and placed there by The Committee of 100.

The **Reuben H. Fleet Space Theater and Science Center** was dedicated March 10, 1973. At 9:00 a.m. the Morse High School, "Marching Tiger Band" directed by Reynaldo V. Vinole Jr., marched from the Palisades area to the Plaza de Balboa for the opening of the festivities. A musical salute by the U.S. Marine Band directed by William Kennedy; the presentation of colors by the U.S. Marine Color Guard under Joseph C. Fegan, Commanding General, followed. The latter were from the San Diego Recruit Depot.

Reuben H. Fleet Space Theater and Science Center

Reuben H. Fleet

The building is of Spanish Colonial design. The larger octagonal section houses the Space Theater. Walls are plain, relieved as the sides converge, and at each central upper portion. Roof treatment shows Spanish Mediterranean tile of reddish brown, a tower accentuated by a decorative frieze crowned with an ornate sculptured finial. Arches lined with fine moulding grace the lower east section. The effect of woven lace of the parapet is crowned with recurring finials.

Inside, the building is modern as the Space Age; pillars of blue ceramic tile, and carpet of blue and ground color. The building is the design of Louis Bodmer, who, with a historian's zeal, may be proudly related back as an associate of William Templeton Johnson: architect, of the San Diego Museum of Art, of the Natural History Museum, (directly to the north) and of the Junípero Serra Museum.

The spreading ficus tree, on the entrance lawn, was planted during the preparation for the 1935 California Pacific Exposition.

This great new addition to Balboa Park was nearly a quarter of a century in becoming a reality. In the 1940s there was "talk" of a Hall of Science and Industry. In 1947 was a suggestion of installing a planetarium in one of the old park buildings. On March 20th, 1957 a meeting was held in the San Diego Hotel at which Robert McPherson acted as chairman. The primary purpose of this meeting was to encourage interest in mathematics among students. At first the thinking seemed to envision two organizations—a Hall of Science and a Planetarium; these two ideas were subsequently combined as one goal.

From 1960, when the city council recognized the benefit of a "Hall of Science and Industry" in San Diego, to the creation of the San Diego Planetarium Authority, to the sale of revenue bonds to finance the construction, to the dedication, on March 10, 1973, the plans went steadily to accomplishment. Now San Diego can proudly proclaim an institution of education, of science, of entertainment, second to none in this country. The name, Reuben H. Fleet, will be immortalized and placed with those of other men and women who have made their names indelible in the history of Balboa Park. For the Space Theater, Major Fleet and his family gave $400,000, matched by the same amount from the Fleet Foundation. Reuben H. Fleet was born in Montesano, Washington (still a territory) in 1887, served in the Washington State Legislature, served in 1917 as an aviator at North Island, was chief of Aviation Training from 1918 till the armistice. He personally inaugurated the first aerial mail service May 15, 1918. In 1923 he organized Consolidated Air-

Interior of
the Reuben H.
Fleet Space Theater

craft Corporation in Rhode Island, moved to Buffalo and finally brought the company to San Diego in 1935. In 1944 he became president of the Institute of Aeronautical Sciences.

His local civic contributions were notable: assistance in securing government subsidies in such projects as Linda Vista, Harbor Drive, and expanded Lindbergh Field; he spearheaded the construction of the community sewage disposal plant, he worked to bring Colorado River water to this county. He provided many scholarships to deserving youth.

In addition to the Fleet Family and Foundation gifts, donations have been received from many other sources. Thus this facility becomes a monument to consecrated community effort.

Park Gardens

North of the former park nursery a large **Rose Garden** has been built. Eventually it will be extended east and almost doubled in size. Back of a fountain in the garden is a plaque dedicating the garden to the memory of Grant Parker and stating that the garden was made possible by the Parker Foundation with assistance from a list of donors. The date is 1975. In this area in November, 1976 an olive tree was donated to the city of San Diego by the Greek Community.

North of the foot bridge crossing Park Boulevard a **Desert Garden** is well started with many unique plants and trees indigenous to the desert.

The **Formal Garden** was established for the first exposition. A wide variety of flowers such as calendulas, zinnias, asters, marigolds, canna, etc. are found here, while rose beds border the northeast and south side of the garden. Hedges of boxwood and myrtle surround the beds. Two rubber trees are located in the area and in the center of the garden is the spreading Moreton Bay Fig Tree, a type of rubber tree which is described under ''Plants and Trees of the Park.'' This garden is located north of the Natural History Museum.

The **Gardenia Garden** is located south of the House of Hospitality. The architect, Richard S. Requa who remodeled the buildings for the second exposition, copied ideas for the building, and the garden from the castle and the gardens of Casa del Rey Moro at Rondo, Spain (House of the Spanish and Moorish Kings). He made the fountains, the grotto, terrace, pergola and plantings all similar to those of this famous Spanish landmark. The garden is bounded at the south by the beautiful pepper tree which shades the Wishing Well.

Water for the fountains is used over and over again. It flows originally from the fountain in the patio of the House of Hospitality through the top and second levels, coming out through the lion's mouth on the lowest level, and from there is pumped back to start over again. The three levels of the gardens are planted with pepper trees, boxwood, hedges, camellias, eugenia, begonias, and Italian cypress. The flower beds are changed seasonally with pansies, marigolds, petunias, snapdragons and other flowers. In the patio of the House of Hospitality are large oriental plants, the giant Bird of Paradise, banana trees and others. Begonias bloom in the patio the year around. The fountain steps and other masonry are patterned after the original garden, as is the handsome wrought iron grill work.

The **Camellia Gardens** are located south of the organ pavilion where gardens of begonias also bloom the year round. In 1951, the Camellia Society planted 500 plants in the canyon south of the House of Hospitality. At present, camelias are found flourishing near the south and west terraces of the House of Hospitality and along the south border of El Prado.

The **Cactus Garden** had been located to the west of the Balboa Park Club, however at present, there is little care given to the garden and it may be abandoned. Some cactus may be moved to the new desert garden east of Park Boulevard.

The **Mall South of El Cid** is a lovely area, grassy in the center, and along the sides is showy throughout the year. In August there are gold and orange hues in shades of marigold; in September salvia is planted by the hundreds, their red blossoms lasting over the holidays.

Flowering Peach Trees covered with beautiful pink bloom in early spring and summer, are located west of Cabrillo Bridge and north of Laurel Street.

The **Zoro Garden** is a sunken shady space east of the Casa de Balboa. It was a show place during the 1935 Exposition; during World War II it was a recreation center for hospital patients. In recent years young actors and musicians have performed here. It has been renovated with new walks, hand rails and plantings to create a walking or theatre type of garden.

The **Alcazar Garden** was created for the 1915 Exposition, and originally was called the Montezuma Garden. In 1935 it was laid out by the Requa-Perry team, and patterned after the gardens surrounding the Alcazar Castle in Seville, Spain which were destroyed during the Spanish Civil War. The ornate fountains are of Moorish style with turquoise blue, yellow and green tiles. The benches and cement arches were 1936 additions to the gardens. A path leads to the south down into Palm Canyon. Flowers are planted in rectangular beds surrounded by boxwood hedges, and defined by symmetrical paths. The beds are filled with calendulas and snapdragons in spring and with zinnias for the fall season.

In 1962 the San Diego Rotary Club celebrated the 50th anniversary of the founding of the club by arranging with the city to renovate the Alcazar Garden. Ferdinand Fletcher was president of the club and his brother Stephen was made chairman of the project. After the city laid new water lines the club installed new sidewalks, a sprinkler system and repaired two fountains in the garden, spending in all nearly $10,000. When the work was finished, July 12, 1962, 300 Rotarians attired in coveralls and caps of the painter ("for fun and Sun") enjoyed box lunches at long tables set in the garden.

The name engraved on the right end of the stage, Beta Sigma Phi is the source of a story of additional generous giving to Balboa Park. A group of women representing the twenty-five San Diego chapters of Beta Sigma Phi International Sorority offered to build the garden stage provided in the Master Plan for the Alcazar Garden. Natalie Steed was in charge of the project for these women who wished to use money left over from conducting a National Convention in San Diego. The city accepted the offer and provided for the necessary excavation. The Callahan Brothers who built the stage were modest in charging for that work. The sorority paid $1677.68. And so, all working together the stage was built; this completed the renovation of Alcazar Garden.

At the location, November 17, 1963 Dr. Frank Lowe gave the invocation; Walter W. Ross founder of the Beta Sigma Phi International made the presentation and Richard Bowen of the Park and Recreation Commission accepted the gift for the city. Stephen Fletcher represented the Rotary Club and Frank Gibson attended for the County Board of Supervisors.

The **Japanese Friendship Garden** will please many San Diegans who regretted the passing of the Japanese Tea House and Garden from the 1915 exposition. That charming little styled house, reached through a gate and red lacquered bridge, was taken down at the end of World War II when the area became part of the Children's Zoo.

In 1956 with the late President Dwight D. Eisenhower's People to People program Sister Cities were begun and the San Diego-Yokohama Sister City Society was one of the first on the west coast. Beginning in the early 1960s that group began formulating specific plans for a garden. In 1968 a site was selected and the Charles C. Dail Memorial Japanese Gate was erected north of the organ pavilion. The project has received approval from the city and awaits only a successful finance campaign for the start of this attractive addition to Balboa Park.

The Trees And Plants of Balboa Park

Beginning from the earliest cultivation of the park, seeds and plants have been introduced from every continent of the world, save Antarctica.

The plants in the park are as cosmopolitan as the visitors. Balboa Park is noted for its great beauty, and this is no accident; Charles B. Harbison of the Natural History Museum has said that landscape architecture was ever the dominant motive in the planting of the park. Australia has contributed more plants to the park than has any other country; the climate there is similar to that of California. The eucalyptus trees are all natives of Australia and many varieties are in the park, including those with naked trunks and lemon scented leaves. Many of the plants and trees from Australia have names which seem at odds with the plant characteristics. This may be accounted for by the fact that when Australia was colonized by Englishmen, they remembered the looks and names of trees and plants from England. Finding similar growths in the new land, they gave English names to them, even though some of these are very superficial. A pine tree comes from Australia that is not a pine tree. Although it looks like a coniferous tree, it is a cunningham beefwood tree. It bears cone-like fruit and is really a narrow-leafed, broad-leafed tree because its leaves are microscopic in size. The Australian silk oak and the she oak are not true oaks. The bottle brush is another tree from Australia, its red flowers resembling bottle brushes.

The camphor tree is an oriental. Several such trees are located in the north west corner of the Formal Garden, north of the Natural History Museum and may be identified by bright green leaves which smell of camphor.

The orchid tree is another oriental; it is not really an orchid tree, but the tree is a type of bean tree. The hydrangea is from Asia, a native of China. The Boston ivy is from Japan and China. An African plant called smilax is a kind of asparagus, and belongs to the lily family.

The cork oaks come from Europe, and the warty bark is a temptation to knife-wielding visitors. The largest tree of this type is guarded by a wire fence and was planted by horticulturist Kate Sessions.

There are two kinds of pepper trees from South America. In Mexico these same trees are called Peru trees because they come from there. There have been known cases when the seeds of the California pepper have been used as an adulterant. A native shrub called the California

*Balboa Park
Nursery, 1954*

holly, is really the christmas berry. Its bright red berries are loved by birds, and have been eaten as food by Indians.

During the first exposition, Sir Thomas Lipton introduced tea trees from Ceylon; others have been planted in the zoo area. However, it seems doubtful if any of these trees remain. There are the Australian tea trees however and from the leaves of this tree tea may be brewed. Something which passes for coffee may be made from the New Zealand coposma. The lemonade berry which grows native in the park has been used by Indians to make a drink by washing the berries in water and producing something which tasted like lemonade.

Among the chaparral in Balboa Park may be found the Holly Leaf cherry. The fruit, which looks like a cherry, has a similar taste; it is edible and has a very large stone. An evergreen Cherry tree comes from Catalina Island; a fan palm from Guadalupe Island; the Poke berry comes from Paraguay in South America. Of the one hundred or so eucalyptus trees introduced into California, twenty-five are most prevalent in the Park.

There are twenty kinds of acacia trees; thirty-five coniferous trees, including the rare Torrey pines. The dammar pine has broad leaves instead of pine needles. There are twenty-two types of palm trees and fifteen varieties of rubber trees. The beautiful Moreton Bay fig tree is related to the India rubber tree, and is a native of Queensland, Australia. Small children call this tree the animal tree, or the Monster tree, and they see in the spreading great roots a semblance of the snake, the elephant and other imagined creatures. And the children can be seen filling the low, inviting branches.

There is an ornamental avocado tree, and outside the zoo entrance is a macadamia nut tree. In the zoo, also in the Pine Grove Picnic area, are banyan trees which are really a type of fig tree. Others of this same genus have the faculty of sending roots from branches and forming new trunks. Somewhat northeast of the Bowling Green is a thriving grove of redwood trees. Specimens of the *Erythea brandegeei*, introduced by Kate Sessions and T.S. Brandegee of the Natural History Museum from their Mexican plant hunting excursion of 1900 may be seen between the Craft Center, south end of Recital Hall, and the North Wall of the Conference Building. These are tall palm trees, single stemmed with fan shaped leaves. An excellent place to study the trees and plants in the Park is within the Zoo where many are plainly marked, with botanical and common names.

In 1958, Timothy Allen, in charge of gardens, painstakingly attached to the park trees their common and botanical names. But young people being what they are, name plates were difficult to maintain.

Three persons are given credit for the variety and the beautiful arrangement of the trees and plants in the park—Kate Sessions, Harry Wegeforth and John Morley.

Balboa Park Cactus Garden, 1935

Other Features Of The Park

Balboa Park is abundantly supplied with many **Picnic Areas** complete with tables and benches in almost every area. Along the west side, on week days at noon dozens of workers from nearby offices may be seen carrying a brown bag as they hurry to a favorite retreat for a restful lunch break. The Morley Field area has received especial attention from the park department. Irrigation has been installed, there is more vegetation; tables and benches were added. Some are so placed that activities may be seen while enjoying a picnic lunch. They may be found near the bocci court, the casting pool, baseball fields and velodrome (bicycle tract).

At present the picnic areas established in 1947-48 are still in use:

ARBOR GROVE: This is on the west side of Pershing Drive and south of Redwood Street—fireplaces and tables can accommodate a fairly large number of people.

GRAPE STREET: Is found at Eighth and Grape Street and late improvements have added rest rooms, and a drinking fountain.

PINE GROVE: This is reached by Balboa Park Drive, south of Laurel or El Prado. The location is southeast of Eighth Avenue Drive and Juniper Street. This popular picnic ground has fireplaces, tables, rest rooms and a drinking fountain. It overlooks Cabrillo Freeway, and dates from 1948. In addition, tables have been set east of South Balboa Park Drive, nearer Laurel Street, and on either side of North Balboa Park Drive are numerous tables, with water, drinking fountains and rest rooms near-by.

GOLDEN HILL: This area was the first to be developed of any of the Balboa Park picnic areas, due to outstanding leadership and community organization among the residents. The groves of Aleppo Pines from Syria and the Italian Stone Pines were set out along the skyline paths, and edging deep canyons. At the head of a ravine on the west side, a circular basin-type fountain, made of porphyry, is known as "The Spring."

The Community Center is in constant use. The children's playground contains many kinds of apparatus. There are asphalt covered basketball courts, two horseshoe courts, and a baseball diamond. This city playground has a full program of activities; it is open during summer vacations from early morning until nine or ten at night. During the school year, it is open after school and at night.

In 1947, the roof of the recreation building burned, and the repair of this started a three-year improvement program. The street leading into the area was widened to create additional parking space, and much landscaping was done in front of the center. Other facilities were enlarged and improved, and a new recreation building was eventually constructed.

In 1972-73 the roads in Golden Hill were realigned, a new irrigation system was installed and there was new landscaping.

This part of Balboa Park is entered from A and Twenty-Eighth Streets or from Twenty-Sixth Street road. It adjoins the Municipal Golf Course.

PEPPER GROVE is situated west of Park Boulevard. The name stems from the pepper trees found chiefly in the south part of the picnic area. This was first developed in 1910 and, after its use during the first exposition and the First World War, the Girl Scouts were located in the area, beginning in 1930. They moved away during the 1935-36 exposition, and the Second World War. During this time a Marine division was stationed here. After the war the Girl Scouts used two buildings in Pepper Grove, one had been donated by Mrs. George C. Burnham. When the Girl Scouts moved to their permanent location in 1955, that building was moved also, and is now called Burnham Hall.

In August 1938, through a project initiated by the Federation of State Societies, a request was made for donations of tables and benches of different sizes, for a cement dance floor, and for a band pavilion for Pepper Grove. The labor for the project had been approved by the W.P.A. and would cost nothing. The material for the bandstand cost $596, the dance floor $400, the small tables and benches $12.50, and the large ones $32. Donations came in for the floor and bandstand, and many individuals and societies built tables and benches. The project was completed during 1938. The bandstand and the dance floor have been removed. Many tables and benches are grouped about. One can imagine the happy evenings spent in the Pepper Grove from 1939 until the Second World War. Music was afforded by the W.P.A. Music Project with many San Diegans enjoying this community accomplishment—an outcome of the efforts of many.

Pepper Grove has excellent picnic facilities. There are swings for children as well as all manner of play apparatus. In 1967 the Thursday Club with the Junior members donated play and climbing equipment. A canyon to the west has been partially filled, its slope was landscaped. Three acres more of lawn were added, new pepper trees were planted, new concrete tables installed. New rest rooms have been added and a cement circled, tiny tots play area. The entrance is now from Park Boulevard.

The **Small Children's Play Area** with modern slides, whirls, swings and other enticing attrac-

Children's Playground, Sixth Avenue

Balboa Park Golf Course, 1954

tions for little children is found at Thorn and
Sixth Avenue. Restrooms nearby are child size,
tables and benches accommodate the adults
watching over. This is an exceedingly popular
family area of the park.

Located north of El Prado and east of Balboa
Drive are two regulation 120 x 120 foot **Bowling
Greens** on which thirteen games may be played
simultaneously. Other facilities include a Club
House with dressing rooms, washrooms, and a
kitchen plus a storage room. The courts were
built in 1932 by the city, and the Club House was
added in 1935 as a W.P.A. Project. The Bowling
Club was organized on July 11, 1932. It is governed by an Executive Board which must ap-
prove all new members. The Club holds
membership in the American Lawn Bowling
Association.

The Balboa Roque Shuffleboard Club was
organized in 1918 to provide and to promote
recreation for persons over fifty through such
games as Shuffleboard, Roque, Chess,
Checkers, Bridge and other card games. Clinton
J. Lester was one of the most devoted and
tireless workers in promoting this center. A club
house was built in 1930 with improvements added in 1931, and in 1934 a second story was added. The club boasted a membership of 1,000 at
this time.

When preparations got under way for the
cross town freeway, the Center had to be
demolished. A new center was established at
Sixth and Ivy, at a cost of $112,000, and was
dedicated February 16, 1961. Mayor Dail cut the
ribbon and Mrs. Merle McPherson was Chairman of the Dedication Committee; Architect
Robert Fowble and Contractor Bill Martens
were present. Civic leaders attending were
Chester Schneider, George Kerrigan, Ross
Tharp, Dr. Frank Lowe and Ivor de Kirby;
representing the park were Pauline des Granges
and Les Earnest.

The building has two large meeting rooms, a
reading room, a kitchen, and Shuffleboard and
Roque courts adjacent to the building. Fur-
niture for the Center was donated by the Junior
League, the *San Diego Union* and the *Evening
Tribune;* the Benbough Furniture Company, the
San Diego and the Hillcrest Lions Clubs;
Members of the Clubs brought stamp books,
pooled them, and purchased needed equipment.

The Redwood Roque Shuffleboard Club
began with roque courts built in 1922; shuffleboard courts were added and the club house
was added in the late forties. At the end of 1968
the clubhouse was in the process of enlargement
and remodelling. Here are located fifteen shuffleboard and six roque courts. Night lighting
was provided in the 1950s. In the clubhouse,
members enjoy chess, checkers, and all types of

Kearns Pool "Learn To Swim Program," 1950s

card games, with bridge the most popular.

The shuffleboard and the Roque Clubs have large and active memberships and offer outdoor activity with lively competition. This center, like the Balboa Clubhouse is located in an area surrounded by beautiful trees, adequate parking is available and the bus line is only two blocks away.

When the plans for the 1915 exposition were made a reality, the golf course located north of the Natural History Museum and established by a private group, was relinquished for the fair's use. Another spot to the south and east was cleared of rock, and a nine-hole **Balboa Park Golf Course** was established. It had sandtraps, greens, and an almost insurmountable hazard called the Rockpile. This course proved very popular and a clamor grew for improvement.

On September 1, 1919, the Park Commission took over the control of the Golf Course. It was resurveyed, and the next year it was extended to eighteen holes. In 1933, activated partly by the desire to create work relief, the citizens of San Diego voted a $111,000 bond issue for the development of the present courses. The Club House was built with W.P.A. labor, and was opened on August 4, 1934. The re-sodding of the course, which had been started in 1931, was finished at this time also. The Club House is equipped with showers, a golf shop, lunch stand, and a lounge. There are golf clubs for men and women, and a golf pro is in charge. The nine-hole golf course had a yardage of 3,372, while the eighteen-hole course yardage is 6,304. The golf course may be reached from two entrances—at Twenty-Eighth and Date Streets,

124

and from Twenty-Sixth and B Streets. Also there is a side road entrance east of Pershing Drive.

Morley Field Sports Complex honors John Morley, park director 1911-1939. This area of Balboa Park was developed over a period of many years. During the depression it furnished many jobs under the W.P.A. Located near the intersection of Texas and Upas Streets, it can be reached from the "Prado" by Park Boulevard north to Morley Drive and east. A new Clubhouse for the Shuffleboard Courts has been added. Among the sports found here are: Tennis, Baseball, Swimming, Bocci and Shuffleboard. San Diegans can be proud of the Tennis Stadium completed in 1970. A Clubhouse was finished about the same time.

Kearns Pool is of tile construction and the water is completely filtered during each eight-hour period. In the service building for the pool and over the office window a plaque honors the namesake, Kearns, a recreation superintendent from 1928-48.

North of the tennis courts and pool, an irrigation system was installed and there is a shady, grassy area with picnic tables.

In 1947, a survey was made by the San Diego Lions Club to determine what was the most needed facility for the blind of the City. Results showed, without a doubt, that a meeting place as a center for activities was uppermost on the list. Thirty thousand dollars were appropriated by the Lions Club.

On June 30, 1948, the Lions Club was given permission by the city to build a **Blind Recreation Center** on a plot 110 by 170 feet, in the park at a location south of Upas Street and east of Park Boulevard, shaded by tall eucalyptus trees with an area for parking. The center opened in 1949, as a non-profit organization for the blind.

Through drives and many donations, the Center organization soon repaid the entire debt, and now the Center is owned and operated by a Board of Directors, three-fourths of whom are made up of blind persons. Twice the building has been enlarged in order to meet the needs of a steadily growing membership. From the original membership of forty, the organization has now reached more than one hundred fifty who pay annual dues. However, all blind persons in the county are welcome to participate in all of the activities offered, and about 400 are involved in some way.

In 1972, the Blind Center received from the California State Department of Rehabilitation a grant for training of the blind. This attitude of helping the individual to lead a more normal life is a great stride over the original aim—a place of recreation. However this needed phase is not neglected.

Boy Scout Headquarters
in Balboa Park

The center is a limited record depository for the talking book machines (record players). White canes are provided when needed, these are supplied by the Lions Club. Many volunteers serve the blind center. They furnish transportation, act as hostesses and help in providing the entertainment.

The **Boy Scouts** were organized in San Diego on October 28, 1910. After the 1915-16 exposition, the scouts were given the use of the Indian Village, built by the Santa Fe Railroad company and used for the portrayal of tribal life. Representatives of the Taos and Zuni tribes had lived there during the Fair. During the First World War, the Scouts moved out and the Indian Village was used by the 21st Artillery. In 1927, the Indian Village was rehabilitated by means of $35,000, which was raised by public subscription. A swimming pool was added, a mess hall and showers were installed. But by 1946, the Indian Village was deemed unsafe for use, and the *San Diego Union* of July 18, 1946, carried the news that the structures, built at a cost of $150,000 were being burned by the Fire Department, and that the area would be landscaped.

On January 2, 1947, it was reported that a fifteen-acre plot in the northwest corner of Balboa Park would be made into an outdoor camp for the Boy Scouts. Contributions of materials or cash were requested. The first buildings would be three sets of double wash houses and a stage building, together with a bowl to seat five hundred boys. And on August 29, 1948, the facilities were installed; the trees were planted—300 in all—and over the stage in a space more than 30 feet long and 8½ feet wide, the Boy Scout Court of Honor had its oath painted.

How this area became the idyllic setting it presents today, is the story of the efforts of many leading citizens, but one name stands out as the master mind of the project, Harvey Atherton. He set out the trees which now stand straight and tall and form a beautiful screen about the grounds. Mr. Atherton had many contacts and he used every one to secure help for his pet interest—the Boy Scouts. He knew of a battleship being dismantled in a northern city, and he secured much of its lumber and had it shipped to San Diego. In the Club House, the beautiful oak floors, fastened down with wooden pegs, are from this battleship.

The Navy gave many surplus benches to the Scouts who in turn shared these with their next door neighbors, the Girl Scouts. In the park, an old building was to be demolished. This was given to the Scouts. Restored, with a shake roof, it fills an urgent need in the fast growing work of this organization.

The observation has been made that men who devote weekends to leading boy scouts on expeditions represent the very finest citizens in the community. Certainly the boy scout program is extremely valuable for training of character and skills. Watching and helping each member of a troop develop desirable traits must bring satisfaction which keeps such men in the program year after year.

The San Diego **Girl Scouts** organization dates back to 1917, the year of the beginning of the First World War for the United States. San Diego had the first Girl Scout Council on the west coast. On January 1, 1930, the organization was loaned two buildings and headquarters were established in Pepper Grove, Balboa Park. One of these buildings was later bought by Mrs. George Burnham and donated to the Girl Scouts. It was later moved, and is now in the present Girl Scout location on Upas Street, where it wears the proud name of Burnham Hall. The San Diego Council embraces Imperial County as well.

In May, 1955, the City Council set aside 6.6 acres for the Girl Scouts in an area bordering Upas and Richmond Streets, and to the west of Roosevelt Junior High School. Aside from Burnham Hall mentioned earlier, all of the buildings, costing more than $142,150, have come from funds that the Girl Scouts had made while selling cookies, or from private donations. These headquarters in Balboa Park are shared equally by the Imperial County girls. Balboa Park offers a beautiful setting for this camp, excelled by few, if indeed any, sites for headquarters. Nearly 6,000 volunteers serve the Girl Scout program in the two counties. Three additional camp sites were built through money provided by the combined efforts of the Girl Scouts.

The Campfire Girls were first organized in San Diego in 1912; the Council was formed in 1927 and was chartered in 1929. Now open to both boys and girls, the organization is simply known as **CampFire.** They were the first located in Balboa Park in an area on the north side of Morley Field where rest rooms are now located. There they leased a little cottage which they named Loligro Cabin (lodge in a little grove). They occupied this campsite in 1937.

During World War II, Loligro Cabin became a Recreational Retreat for the Army. After the war ended, the Campfire Girls again had the site from 1946 to 1957. In the latter year, a lease of six acres was secured on the east side of Balboa Park Drive and east of Quince to Upas Streets. Here, the group owns a caretaker's cottage and rest room facilities.

The area bounded by Upas Street on the north, on the east by Morley Field, on the south and southeast by Pershing Drive, and on the west by the Naval Hospital and Park Boulevard is known as **Florida Canyon.** The size of the area described is considered to be between 100 and 150 acres. Aside from busy Florida Street bisecting the canyon from north to south, and the U.S. Naval Hospital buildings, it is a native portion of Balboa Park. To all who love the park and the history of it, Florida Canyon represents the park as it was seen by Samuel Parsons when he came out from New York on December 21, 1902, to begin planning and shaping the park. His description of this choice area, sent to New York papers, is recorded in an earlier chapter. Too, George Marston loved the native plants, which were all that was here, when he first saw the park. He describes, in his writing, the wildflowers he found on his walks. Many of the same flowers may be seen today. One looks back over the years to the time when E.W. Morse and Alonzo Horton selected these acres, to be "forever for a park." Some officials say this natural growth is typical of a San Diego canyon of 500 years ago.

The Administration Of Balboa Park

Within recent years many improvements have been made in the park. New irrigation systems have enabled green lawns to replace barren ground, areas of dense growth and underbrush have been cleared. There is little trash to mar the beauty. Often visitors comment on the immaculate park, especially about what large areas which must be maintained.

The programs within the park and the maintenance over the park are the function of the Park and Recreation Department. The structural maintenance is done by the Park Maintenance Division, also a part of the Park and Recreation Department.

There is a voluntary Park and Recreation Board, members being appointed by the City Council and serving for two years or more, but not longer than the term of the Mayor under whom they were appointed, or until they are replaced. This Committee of eleven members is chosen for experience in community affairs or for some particular interest, talent or capacity. They are chosen to some extent according to Council districts although this is not necessarily so. The function of this committee is purely advisory, and it brings to the Council through the City Manager, specific needs of the park and the recreation problems of their various communities.

The Chairman of the Park and Recreation Board chooses a number of sub-committees. An example would be the Balboa Park Committee, composed of members of several groups with the specific aims of protecting and improving the park. Other committees are less active and may be called on only when a problem arises which needs special consideration.

The Future

Someone wrote that during the Panama-California Exposition the significance of the architecture of the buildings, though noted, was never appreciated as it became in the following years. Now in San Diego the architecture is treasured because it probably represents the finest example of a period, Spanish Renaissance, of any group of buildings in the world.

The Balboa Park Citizens Study Committee of 1957 leaves these thoughts on the care of the precious acres:

"The preservation for over forty years of many of the 1915 Exposition Buildings despite the fact that they were originally constructed of wood frame and stucco as 'temporary buildings' for a one-year life expectancy, indicates the reverenced place these structures hold in the admiration and affection of San Diegans and visitors from all over the world. When one reviews the impermanent nature of certain of these structures and the fact that many of them have known no practical use for extended periods of their existence, we have proof beyond a doubt that their outstanding beauty has endowed them with a degree of permanence not inherent in their structure.

That our primarily practical people have

for so long been deeply moved and attracted by the beauty of the composite of buildings and gardens in Balboa Park, is proof positive that all future development must be directed to continue this aesthetic masterpiece through carefully considered maintenance and development.

To the thousands of citizens who wish to retain Balboa Park in all its beauty and to many of those citizens who dread the removal of a single beautiful old structure, we call attention to the fact that the immutable hand of time and decay will sooner or later destroy each of the temporary structures. The greatest tribute therefore which we can pay to this center of civic culture, will be to initiate and with perseverance carry on a continuing program of development in Balboa Park, which will insure that as each old structure passes into memory it will be replaced with buildings and/or gardens of commensurate beauty, blended into the inspired design concept of the original group of 1915 Exposition Buildings and gardens.

Our generation is passing to the future a heritage of astoundingly expanded economy devoted primarily to the practical aspects of our civilization. Compounded with this we pass on massive debt and a seeming disregard for the preservation of many natural resources. It is our profound duty, therefore, that we pass intact to the future, Balboa Park, this transcendant work of the hands of men, some of whom have passed on and some of whom are still present in our day."

By Samuel Wood Hamill, AIA

*Casa de Balboa
under construction,
November, 1980*

Bibliography

Amero, Richard W. "Waiting in Limbo: The History of the Ford Building in Balboa Park" *The Mason Street Papers,* Vol. 3, 1979.

Amero, Richard W. "The California Building" *The Mason Street Papers,* Vol. 10, 1981.

Amero, Richard W. Personal Scrapbook, The History of Balboa Park.

Benton, F. Weber. *Semi-Tropical California.* L.B. Benton Publishing Company, 1915.

Black, Samuel F. *History of San Diego County.* Chicago: S.J. Clarke Publishing Company, 1913.

Britton, James. "Art of the City: Heed the Voices and Save the Park" *San Diego Magazine,* Vol. 13, December, 1960.

Davidson, G. Aubrey. History of the California Expositions. San Diego Historical Society Research Archives.

Dapprich, Fred. "George W. Marston" *Westways,* Vol. 26, July, 1923.

Ervine, Sam. "The 1935 Exposition" *San Diego Magazine,* Vol. 17, June, 1965.

Hagberg, Marilyn. "El Prado" *San Diego Magazine,* Vol. 20, February, 1968.

Heilbron, Carl H., ed. *History of San Diego County.* San Diego Press Club, 1936.

Hewett, Edgar Lee and Johnson, William Templeton. "Panama-California Exposition, 1915" *Papers of the School of American Archaeology,* No. 32, April 1916.

Hewett, Edgar. "Ancient America at the Panama-California Exposition, 1915" Reprinted from *The Theosophical Path,* February, 1915

Horn, Robert L. "City Park Gets a Name" *California Garden,* Vol. 51, Autumn, 1960.

James, George Warton. *Exposition Memories.* Pasadena: Radiant Life Press, 1917.

Jerabek, C.I. "Plant Life in Balboa Park" *Municipal Employee,* Vol. 7, September, 1938.

McGroarty, John Steven. "San Diego Pageant" *West Coast Magazine,* Vol. 2, October 1911.

MacPhail, Elizabeth C. *Kate Sessions: Pioneer Horticulturist.* San Diego: San Diego Historical Society, 1976.

MacPhail, Elizabeth C. *The Story of New San Diego and of its Founder Alonzo E. Horton.* San Diego: San Diego Historical Society, 1979.

Montes, Gregory. "San Diego City Park, 1868-1902: An Early Debate on Environment and Profit" *The Journal of San Diego History,* Vol. 23, Spring, 1977.

Montes, Gregory. "San Diego's City Park, 1902-1910: From Parsons to Balboa" *The Journal of San Diego History,* Vol. 25, Winter, 1979.

Montes, Gregory. "Balboa Park, 1909-1911: The Rise and Fall of the Olmsted Plan" *The Journal of San Diego History,* Vol. 27, Winter, 1982.

Perry, W. Allen. *History of Balboa Park.* San Diego Park and Recreation Department.

Pourade, Richard F. *History of San Diego.* 7 Vols. San Diego: Union-Tribune Publishing Company, 1960-1977.

Quinn, James Miller. *History and Biographical Record of Southern California.* Chicago: Chapman Publishing Company, 1902.

Requa, Richard S. *Inside Lights on the Buildings of the San Diego Exposition, 1935-1937.* San Diego Historical Society Research Archives.

San Diego Historical Society Research Archives. Biographical Files, Miscellaneous Books and Manuscripts.

San Diego Public Library. California Room. Miscellaneous Books, Documents and Manuscripts.

Smythe, William E. *History of San Diego, 1542-1908.* San Diego: The History Company, 1908.

Stewart, Don M. *Frontier Port.* Los Angeles: The Ward Richie Press, 1965.

Thornbaugh, Margaret. "San Diego's Wonderful Park" *Westways,* Vol. 52, May, 1960.

Trembley, Ralph. *Balboa Park—What's In It.* San Diego Park and Recreation Department Publication, 1967.

Wagner, Harr, Publisher. *Golden Era Magazine.* Miscellaneous issues.

Wangenheim, Julius. "The Autobiography of Julius Wangenheim" *California Historical Society Quarterly,* Vol. 5, June, 1956.

Index